DRESSED

BLUE PLATE
MAYONNAISE
BLUE PLATE
STEEL

DRESSED

100 Years of Blue Plate Mayonnaise *and the* Foodways of the Gulf South

83 press®

83 press

Published by 83 Press, an imprint of
Hoffman Media, LLC.
Birmingham, Alabama
www.83press.com

ISBN 978-1-971708-04-1
Printed in USA

Photography by Denny Culbert

Additional photography
by Ryan Hodgson-Rigsbee
(pages 4-5, 58-59, 150, 151, 228-229, 250-251)

DEDICATION

To the families, neighbors, restaurants,
and grocers that kept Blue Plate
at their tables and on their shelves
for 100 years, thank you.

To the makers, growers, bakers, and
family brands who've been a part
of every memorable meal, it's an
honor to be in such good company.

Blue Plate has always lived where
food is shared, stories are told, and
everyone lingers a little longer.

We're grateful to have been part
of your traditions and are
inspired by your joie de vivre.

Cheers to the next 100!

Contents

Water made New Orleans possible. Defined by the Mississippi River Delta, the city has drawn generations of people who influenced the region's distinctive culinary traditions to its shores. It's where Blue Plate Mayonnaise debuted and grew to become an enduring favorite in kitchens throughout the Gulf South—deliciously flavoring life's moments and memories.

HOME OF JAX BEER

CHAPTER 1

Getting Dressed

In the Gulf South, "dressed" isn't just how you finish a po-boy. It's how you cook, how you feed people; it's even in how you set the table and get yourself ready to invite everyone in to pull up a chair. Dressed means taking the extra step that turns meals into memories. This chapter is about the place, the people, and the ingredient—Blue Plate Mayonnaise—that has been dressing Gulf South tables for a hundred years.

WELCOME IN

Spend any time in the cities and towns that line the Gulf Coast, the Mississippi Delta, the bayous, piney woods, and barrier islands—the Gulf South, if you will—and it quickly becomes clear that food is more than just something to eat. In this place, "getting dressed" is a way of life. It's about bringing a little something extra to everything and turning the ordinary into something memorable. It shapes the rhythms of daily life, marks the seasons, brings people together, and gives communities a shared sense of identity and place.

Iconic dishes and the traditions surrounding them define this region in ways that go far beyond the plate. Red beans and rice became the de facto dish of Monday wash days because a pot could simmer unattended while the chore was done, so embedded in the culture that jazz musician Louis Armstrong signed his personal letters "Red Beans and Ricely Yours." The po-boy arose from an act of generosity and became a symbol of a city and, in time, an entire region. How you order it, "dressed," is as specific and telling as the story behind it (see page 66 to read about that). A fish fry means it's Friday, a boucherie means community as much as it means butchering a hog, and a crawfish boil means the season has arrived and everyone is welcome. Backyard gardens feed the table, and community celebrations and gatherings like Jazz Fest in New Orleans and Mardi Gras showcase beloved dishes like gumbo and crawfish bread. From Louisiana to the Florida Panhandle, from Mobile Bay to the Texas coast, the specifics of the dishes may evolve, but the spirit at the table is the same. And at that table is Blue Plate Mayonnaise—woven into the dishes, and as much a part of the Gulf South table as anything on it.

THE BEGINNING OF BLUE PLATE MAYONNAISE

Blue Plate Mayonnaise debuted in 1927 from a simple idea: A jar of mayonnaise should taste exactly like homemade. The brand was developed by Wesson Oil executive Charles Nehlig, as a way to use the company's oil surplus. After more than a thousand taste tests in real customers' kitchens, it hit grocery store shelves with a name and label inspired by Blue Willow dishware. The popular china pattern was collected in homes and adorned tables throughout the South. It stood for everyday elegance and the grace that comes with gathering and sharing a meal. The place was New Orleans, and from the start, the mayonnaise helped shape the identity and foodways of the city and the region beyond it. What began as a grassroots effort—a handful of salesmen leaving jars at markets—grew to become a bona fide Gulf South institution.

Legacy

In 1943, Blue Plate Mayonnaise production moved into a new factory in New Orleans' Gert Town neighborhood. The gleaming, state-of-the-art building announced that Blue Plate had taken root, in the middle of WWII and against considerable odds no less. Ownership has changed hands over the decades, but since 1974, the mayonnaise has been part of the family-owned Reily Foods Company, which has stewarded the brand for more than half a century. Still made the same way and served by fiercely loyal Gulf South families and chefs, Blue Plate is approaching the start of its second century. In 2024, Louisiana Lt. Governor Billy Nungesser made it official, proclaiming Blue Plate the Official Mayonnaise of Po-Boys. But the Gulf South has known that all along.

Mayonnaise was the flagship of the Blue Plate Foods brand, which expanded to include a diverse line of products. Coffee, preserves, canned vegetables and fruit, jams, peanut butter, and margarine were among the early offerings, and the line grew to over 34 foods sold under the Blue Plate name. By 1949, the brand's reach extended to stores across the South, as far west as San Antonio, Texas, and east to cities like Washington, DC.

Reily Foods acquired the Blue Plate brand in 1974, and the only product to come with the name was the crown jewel: the mayonnaise, which remains a regional favorite.

THIS PAGE: (Above) Vintage mayonnaise label under Wesson Oil; (Below) A vintage International Harvester Blue Plate Mayonnaise delivery truck, circa 1940.

OPPOSITE PAGE: (Top) The Gert Town factory, designed by August Perez Jr., is now home to Blue Plate Artist Lofts, a residential community that supports the local arts community. The building was listed on the National Register of Historic Places in 2008, and the original Blue Plate sign still stands. (Bottom) Vintage Blue Plate ads.

BLUE PLATE
BLUE PLATE
BLUE
PLATE
artist lofts

BLUE PLATE
"pantry"
AT YOUR NEAREST AND NICEST GROCER★

Blue Plate
OKRA and
TOMATOES
A PERFECT MAIN DISH -- AN IDEAL SOUP MIX

KIDS
love it on bread—
good for them too!
BLUE PLATE
MAYONNAISE
at your grocer

FOODWAYS FOUNDATIONS

The food of the Gulf South came from everywhere at once. West African cooks brought rice, okra, and a command of technique. Acadian settlers carried their traditions into the bayous and built a cooking culture rooted in what the land and water provided. In Creole kitchens in New Orleans, French, Spanish, German, African, and Caribbean influences melded into something entirely new. Sicilian immigrants who arrived in Louisiana in the late 19th century left their mark on New Orleans' markets, its food culture, and its tables. Indigenous communities whose knowledge of the land, the plants, and the waters of this region shaped what everyone else would eventually cook.

In the Gulf South, *feeding people well* is not a gesture. It is a way of life.

In the Mississippi Delta, Mexican laborers working alongside African American sharecroppers gave the region its tamale traditions, still found today at roadside stands and gas stations. Vietnamese refugees who settled along the Gulf Coast after 1975 were drawn by the fishing culture and brought a food tradition that has become part of the region's fabric. The Gulf South is a place where many cultures arrived, took root, and changed the food forever. The recipes in this book represent that: layered, generous, and deeply rooted in the people who built this place. Welcome in.

THE KITCHEN WORKHORSE

Mayonnaise plays a central role in the recipes in this book—and for good reason. You'll soon realize it's much more than simply a condiment; rather, it's a versatile workhorse in the kitchen, bringing richness, moisture, and tang while serving as a binder, tenderizer, browning agent, and the foundation for countless dishes.

Watch what happens when you brush mayonnaise on proteins like chicken or a beef roast before browning: The fat in the yolks caramelizes on the protein's surface. As a marinade, it clings and seasons while sealing in moisture. As a binder, it holds crab cakes and croquettes together without heaviness. Taste the richness in dips and dressings where the emulsion step is already complete and leaves you free of complicated technique. Stir it into batters for cakes whose crumb stays remarkably moist and tender for days. Brush it on biscuits before baking, and see it deliver a deep golden finish that an egg wash can't touch.

You'll see exactly *why mayonnaise*, especially Blue Plate Mayonnaise, is one of the hardest working ingredients in the kitchen.

The recipes in this book were created using Blue Plate Mayonnaise. It is the preferred mayonnaise for all the recipes in this book, but it's also our only recommendation in the dishes where fat content and emulsification directly affect the outcome. Its egg yolk–only formula and high fat content create a rich emulsion that can replace or reduce the amount of butter, oil, and other fats in recipes. Some approaches in the recipes will be familiar; others push mayonnaise into new culinary territory. It's a wide range that demonstrates just how versatile mayonnaise is.

Panacea
Sopchoppy
GOD BLESS AMERICA
And PASS THE
TUPELO HONEY

Roadside signs tempt travelers to stop for local specialties like Tupelo honey. Bees gather nectar from the blossoms of white tupelo trees growing in Gulf Coast swamps such as Florida's Apalachicola River basin and the Choctawhatchee River basin, producing one of the Gulf South's most prized honeys.

Food shopping in and around New Orleans is affectionately referred to as "making groceries." Home cooks source ingredients from neighborhood butchers, seafood shops, local produce farmers, and supermarkets to stock up on the week's meals.

PANTRY ESSENTIALS

Beyond stocking a jar of Blue Plate Mayonnaise, you'll want to keep these staples on hand to jump-start your Gulf South cooking journey.

Blackening Seasoning: Built for high heat and cast iron cooking, this blend of paprika, cayenne, and other savory spices creates a deeply flavorful crust that is anything but burnt. Available at most grocery stores or make your own (see page 27).

Cajun Seasoning: Leads with hot, smoky flavor built for bold, rustic cooking. Find it at any grocery store or make your own (see page 27).

Cane Syrup: Pure cane syrup has a deep, rich sweetness with mild molasses notes and is less bitter and more nuanced than standard molasses. Our favorite brand is Steen's 100% Pure Cane Syrup.

Cornmeal: Yellow offers pronounced corn flavor; white is milder and traditional across much of the Deep South. Fine-ground works best for baked goods like cornbread and hush puppies; medium-ground is ideal for dredging; coarse-ground is reserved for grits. Stone-ground provides the fullest flavor but is perishable—store it in the refrigerator or freezer.

Creole Mustard: Traditionally made from coarsely ground brown mustard seeds marinated in vinegar, Creole mustard has a delicate texture and a tangy, sharp bite that sets it apart from standard yellow or Dijon. You'll find it in remoulades, dressings, and sauces throughout the book.

Creole Seasoning: This workhorse of the Gulf South spice cabinet is built on a base of paprika, garlic, onion, oregano, thyme, cayenne, and black pepper. Prepared blends are available at grocery stores or make your own (see page 27).

Holy Trinity: Onion, celery, and bell pepper are the aromatic foundation of Gulf South cooking, appearing in gumbos, braises, rice dishes, and stuffings throughout this book. The standard ratio is 2 parts onion to 1 part each celery and bell pepper. Dice the vegetables uniformly so they cook evenly.

Long-Grain Rice: This rice cooks into light, separate grains, making it the preferred choice for Gulf South cooking. Unless a recipe specifies otherwise, avoid substituting instant rice.

Louisiana-Style Hot Sauce: Made with aged cayenne or tabasco peppers, vinegar, and salt, Louisiana-style hot sauce brings a tangy heat to dishes during cooking and at the table. Brands vary in vinegar brightness and intensity. For the recipes in this book, we recommend a Louisiana brand. Some of our favorites are Crystal, Louisiana, and Tabasco.

Olive Salad: A New Orleans staple of chopped olives, giardiniera, capers, and garlic in olive oil and vinegar is essential to the iconic cold-cut sandwich, the muffuletta. In this book, it brings a salty edge to deviled eggs (see page 144). Look for jarred versions free of preservatives and stabilizers for the brightest, most authentic flavor.

SPICE BLENDS

Invest just a few minutes to mix up your own Gulf South–centric spice blends for maximum flavor. It's easy and well worth it. Start with the freshest ingredients: Check expiration dates and choose quality brands. Once blended, store the mixtures in airtight containers away from heat and light. Like any ground spice or dried herb, potency fades over time, so use the blends often: Stir into beans and braises, rub onto roasts, or mix into softened butter for a delicious compound butter.

Baquet Creole Seasoning

Makes about 2 cups

This seasoning blend comes from Wayne Baquet, Jr., who uses it at Li'l Dizzy's Cafe, a Creole soul food restaurant in New Orleans that he owns and operates with his wife, Arkesha. You may want to try it with Arkesha's recipe, Smothered Pork Chops and Onion Gravy, shared on page 31.

- 1¼ cups fine sea salt
- 3 tablespoons onion powder
- 3 tablespoons garlic powder
- 3 tablespoons cayenne pepper
- 3 tablespoons ground black pepper
- 1½ tablespoons ground white pepper

1. In a medium bowl, combine all ingredients. Store in an airtight container for up to 6 months.

Open the kitchen cabinet of any *good* Gulf South cook, and you'll find the same things: smoke, heat, acid, and depth that can't be rushed.

Blackening Rub

Makes about ¼ cup

- 1 tablespoon Spanish paprika
- 2 teaspoons kosher salt
- 1 teaspoon onion powder
- 1 teaspoon garlic powder
- 1 teaspoon celery salt
- 1 teaspoon dried thyme
- 1 teaspoon dried oregano
- 1 teaspoon cayenne pepper
- 1 teaspoon chipotle pepper
- 1 teaspoon crushed black pepper

1. In a small bowl, combine all ingredients. Store in an airtight container for up to 6 months.

Cajun Spice Mix

Makes about ⅔ cup

- 2 tablespoons kosher salt
- 2 tablespoons garlic powder
- 1 tablespoon onion powder
- 4 teaspoons smoked paprika
- 2 teaspoons ground oregano
- 2 teaspoons ground thyme
- 2 teaspoons ground black pepper
- 1 teaspoon cayenne pepper

1. In a small bowl, combine all ingredients. Store in an airtight container for up to 6 months.

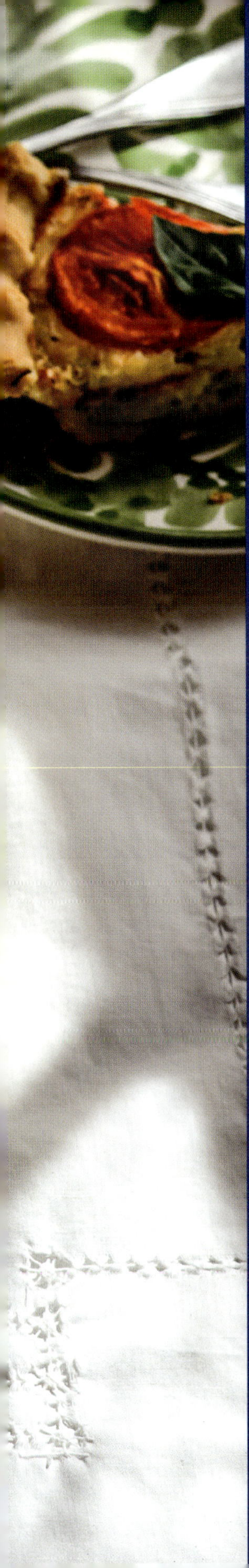

CHAPTER 2

Y'all Come in, Dinner's Ready

These weeknight meals capture the richness of day-to-day life in the Gulf South, where even the simplest meals are steeped in bold flavors and years of tradition. Sustenance is only part of the story; the true spirit is about living to eat. A table set with food this simple and satisfying is worth rushing home to.

CONTRIBUTOR

Arkesha Baquet
Li'l Dizzy's Cafe

Tremé
New Orleans, LA

Arkesha Baquet and her husband, Wayne Baquet, Jr., are keeping family history and food traditions alive at Li'l Dizzy's Cafe, a Creole soul food restaurant in Tremé—New Orleans' oldest African American neighborhood and the birthplace of jazz. Regular menu offerings, like gumbo and fried chicken, and daily specials, like red beans and rice and smothered pork chops, keep the faithful coming back week after week. The restaurant is named for a Baquet grandchild nicknamed Li'l Dizzy, a nod to jazz legend Dizzy Gillespie.

Smothered Pork Chops and Onion Gravy

Makes 6 to 8 servings

Smothered pork chops are the quintessential weeknight dinner across Gulf South kitchens. It's a dish that incorporates some of the West African slow-cooking traditions that shape Louisiana's Creole and Cajun cuisines. The technique is simple: Pork chops are floured and browned and then returned to the skillet to simmer in a rich cooking base that develops into a thick, savory gravy. The delicious result is chops that are practically fall-off-the-bone tender. Modest ingredients become next-level wonderful for a weeknight, but they're also good enough for impromptu company.

Arkesha Baquet's version builds its gravy on onions, garlic, and sweet red bell pepper, with aromatics and spice from a homemade Creole seasoning deepening the flavor. A spoonful of mayonnaise stirred into the gravy at the very end mirrors the French practice of monter au beurre *(dotting with cold butter) at the finish to add body, sheen, and richness. The mayonnaise lends the gravy a subtle creaminess, a background brightness from acidity, and depth. Serve over rice for full appreciation of the rich, flavorful gravy.*

- **6 (½-inch-thick) bone-in pork chops**
- **1½ teaspoons kosher salt**
- **1 teaspoon coarsely ground black pepper**
- **½ cup all-purpose flour**
- **3 tablespoons vegetable oil**
- **½ cup unsalted butter**
- **2 cups chopped yellow onion**
- **½ cup chopped red bell pepper**
- **1 tablespoon finely minced garlic**
- **3 cups chicken stock**
- **2 teaspoons Baquet Creole Seasoning (page 27)**
- **¼ cup Blue Plate Mayonnaise**
- **Cooked white rice or Creamiest Buttermilk Mashed Potatoes (page 55), to serve**
- **Garnish: chopped fresh parsley**

1. Heat a 12-inch cast-iron skillet over medium-high heat. Season pork chops with salt and pepper. Sprinkle the pork all over with flour; set aside any remaining flour.

2. Add oil to skillet. Sear pork chops for 3 to 4 minutes per side until well browned. Remove from skillet, and set aside.

3. Reduce heat to medium. Melt butter in skillet, and stir in reserved flour. Cook, stirring often, until golden brown. (It should be the color of peanut butter.) Add onion, and cook, stirring occasionally, until softened, about 6 to 7 minutes. Add bell pepper, and cook 3 to 5 minutes or until tender. Stir in garlic, and cook until fragrant, about 30 seconds.

4. Gradually whisk in chicken stock until smooth. Stir in Baquet Creole Seasoning.

5. Return pork chops and any reserved juices to skillet, nestling into gravy. Bring to a boil, then reduce heat to low. Cover, and simmer for 1 hour or until tender.

6. Remove pork chops, and keep warm. In a small bowl, whisk together mayonnaise and ¼ cup warm gravy from skillet until smooth; whisk into remaining gravy in skillet. Add pork chops, turning to coat. Remove from heat. Serve with rice or Creamiest Buttermilk Mashed Potatoes. Garnish with parsley, if desired.

Whole Roast Chicken

Makes 6 servings

A stunning centerpiece roast hardly seems possible on a weeknight, but a beautiful whole chicken is a game-changer. With the help of an herbed mayonnaise basting mixture, a simple roast bird is more than attainable: It can become part of your regular rotation. The parsley, thyme, and oregano-scented mayonnaise creates burnished skin that emerges from the oven golden, crisp, and deeply flavorful. Aromatics—garlic, onion, and carrot—stuffed inside the cavity lend moisture and flavor that optimize the chicken's natural savoriness from the inside out. This chicken is easy enough to pull off on a Tuesday night, but also special enough to hold its own at the Sunday dinner table.

- **1 (6-pound) roasting chicken**
- **4 teaspoons kosher salt, divided**
- **1 teaspoon ground black pepper, divided**
- **1 cup Blue Plate Mayonnaise**
- **¼ cup chopped fresh parsley**
- **1 tablespoon chopped fresh thyme**
- **1 teaspoon dried oregano**
- **1 teaspoon smoked paprika**
- **1 onion, peeled and quartered**
- **1 carrot, peeled and quartered**
- **1 celery stalk, quartered**
- **1 small garlic bulb, halved vertically**

1. Line a rimmed baking sheet with foil. Place a wire rack over foil in baking sheet.
2. Thoroughly dry chicken with a paper towel. Season inside and outside of chicken with 2 teaspoons salt and ½ teaspoon pepper. Place on prepared pan and refrigerate uncovered for 1 to 4 hours.
3. Preheat oven to 450°F. In a small bowl, whisk together mayonnaise, parsley, thyme, remaining 2 teaspoons salt, oregano, paprika, and remaining ½ teaspoon pepper.
4. Rub half of mayonnaise mixture on all surfaces of the chicken, coating it completely. Stuff the onion, carrot, celery, and garlic into the cavity. Let stand at room temperature for 15 minutes.
5. Place in center of the oven, and roast for 30 minutes. Reduce heat to 350°F, and continue roasting for 1 hour to 1 hour and 20 minutes, using a rubber spatula to brush more mayonnaise mixture onto chicken until the breast and thigh temperature reaches 165°F to 175°F. If the skin begins to get too dark, remove the chicken, tent it with aluminum foil, and return to the oven. When done, remove the chicken from the oven, and let stand for 15 minutes before carving.

Southern Spins for Roast Chicken

Mayonnaise as a baster for chicken or turkey is a starting point. From there, you can mix it with just about any flavor combination you wish. Try these or follow your instinct and create your own.

- **Smoked paprika and garlic powder:** You'll find these spices in just about every Southern pantry. Use them to add warmth, depth, and color.
- **Creole mustard and thyme:** Create a distinctly Louisiana spin with tangy notes and herbal aroma.
- **Cajun seasoning and lemon zest:** Balance the heat in the Cajun seasoning against the brightness from the citrus.

The best approach is to start small, stirring in ingredients gradually and tasting as you go until the flavor is where you want it. Watch out when using fresh garlic and citrus which can burn easily under direct heat and become bitter. Instead, spread the mayonnaise mixture under the skin. Use liquid-based additions like vinegar, hot sauce, or juice sparingly—a mixture that's too thin won't cling to the skin the way you need it to.

Red beans and rice has been part of New Orleans food culture for more than two centuries, landing in Louisiana pots through the West African, French, Spanish, and Caribbean foodways that shaped Louisiana's cuisine. The dish was often made and served on Monday—wash day—since the slow-simmered beans could cook themselves while the laundry chores were handled. Modern times gave way to faster and simpler household tasks, but the custom of coming together over a Monday pot of red beans and rice continues as a symbol of community and generosity. Two types of red beans are commonly used to make the dish: small, creamy and mildly sweet red beans, the Louisiana standard, or red kidney beans, which are larger with a firm texture and hearty bite.

CONTRIBUTOR

Emily Shaya
Cofounder and Director of New Projects, Pomegranate Hospitality

New Orleans, LA

Emily Shaya, cofounder of Pomegranate Hospitality with her husband, Chef Alon Shaya, has made Monday red beans and rice a regular gathering at her home. And her beans are well worth sitting down to. In 2019, Shaya took her dish to the Krewe of Red Beans' Bean Madness competition—and won—beating out 31 other competitors.

Emily Shaya's Famous Red Beans and Rice

Makes 10 to 12 servings

Red beans and rice can't be rushed. You have to soak the beans ahead, and then let them cook low and slow until they soften and soak up the flavors of the cooking liquid. Emily enriches the braising liquid by starting with fat rendered from bacon; the browned bits that flavor the chicken stock (rather than water) are part of a signature move for her award-winning beans. Toasting the dried spices in the bacon fat deepens their flavor impact.

- 2 pounds dried red beans, soaked overnight
- ¼ cup extra-virgin olive oil
- 6 ounces bacon, chopped
- 2 yellow onions, divided
- 2 stalks celery, chopped
- 1 green bell pepper, chopped
- 2 dried bay leaves, divided
- 1 tablespoon sweet paprika
- ½ teaspoon cayenne pepper
- 1 large smoked ham hock or shank
- 6 cups chicken stock
- 1 pound smoked pork sausage
- 2 teaspoons Morton kosher salt, divided
- 4 teaspoons Tabasco sauce, plus more for serving
- 2 teaspoons sugar
- ½ cup canola oil
- 4 tablespoons unsalted butter
- 1 pound jasmine rice
- 3 cups water, or more as needed
- 1 bunch green onions, sliced
- Skillet Cornbread (page 233), to serve

1. Drain the beans, and set them aside.

2. Warm olive oil in a large heavy-bottomed pot over medium heat. Add bacon; cook, stirring occasionally, to break it up for 6 to 8 minutes or until golden.

3. Meanwhile, chop 1 onion. When most of the bacon's fat has rendered, add the chopped onion to the pot with the celery, bell pepper, and 1 bay leaf, stirring well to coat everything with the fat. Continue to cook, stirring occasionally, until the onion is translucent and the celery and bell pepper just start to soften. Stir in the paprika and cayenne, allowing the spices to toast for a minute or so.

4. Add the beans, ham hock, and stock. Increase the heat to high to bring to a boil, then skim any foam from the top of the pot, reduce the heat to low, and cover with the lid. Let it cook, low and slow, for at least 3 hours, until the beans are falling apart. It's not a soup, but there should be enough broth so that you see some movement in the pot; top it off with more stock if you need to.

5. Fish the ham hock out of the pot, pull the meat off the bone and rough chop, and add it back to the pot; slice the sausage about ¼ inch thick and add that. Season with 1 teaspoon salt, Tabasco, and sugar. Continue to cook, covered, over low heat, for another 30 minutes, until it all starts to pull together. You can leave it alone for a couple of hours, returning just to stir occasionally.

6. While that happens, make the rice: First, chop the remaining onion. Combine canola oil and butter with the remaining bay leaf in a separate pot over medium heat. Once the butter melts, add the onion and remaining 1 teaspoon salt.

7. As soon as the onion is translucent, stir in the rice. Defer to the package instructions for a water ratio; for 1 pound (about 2 cups) jasmine rice, add 3 cups water. Increase the heat to high and bring to a simmer; then decrease the heat to low, cover, and cook for another 15 minutes or so, until it's tender.

8. Remove rice from heat; let rest 10 minutes with lid on, then fluff with a fork. Remove and discard bay leaves from both pots. Serve red beans over a scoop of rice, sprinkle with green onions, and serve with Tabasco and Skillet Cornbread.

Crab Cakes

Makes 4

Crab cakes have a long history along the Gulf Coast, with each coastal community claiming its own version and its own standards. In Mobile, Alabama, crab cake style puts lump crabmeat first and any seasoning or even mayonnaise (which acts as a binder and brings in flavor too) in as a supporting character. It makes sense when the blue crabs caught in the region's inland waterways are sweet, with delicate flavor.

Fresh crabmeat seasoned with Worcestershire, Dijon, salt, and pepper are first shaped into patties, next coated with breadcrumbs, and lastly pan-fried, becoming golden and crisp outside and warm and creamy inside. If you like a little punch, include the minced jalapeño or substitute red bell pepper for an even sweeter outcome. Well suited to almost any remoulade (see pages 206 and 207 for all the possibilities), these crab cakes are paired here with a classic New Orleans remoulade that includes paprika and Worcestershire. Savory and slightly sweet, it's a natural match for the simple crab cakes.

1¼ cups panko (Japanese breadcrumbs), divided
½ cup Blue Plate Mayonnaise
1 large egg yolk, lightly beaten
2 teaspoons fresh lime juice
1 teaspoon Worcestershire sauce
1 teaspoon Dijon mustard
¼ teaspoon kosher salt
¼ teaspoon ground black pepper
8 ounces lump crabmeat, picked free of shell
2 tablespoons finely chopped fresh chives
1 tablespoon finely chopped jalapeño (optional)
2 tablespoons vegetable oil
New Orleans Remoulade (page 206), to serve

1. Line a baking sheet with parchment paper.
2. In a medium bowl, combine ½ cup breadcrumbs, mayonnaise, egg yolk, lime juice, Worcestershire sauce, mustard, salt, and black pepper. Using a rubber spatula, gently stir in crabmeat, chives, and jalapeño, if desired.
3. Place remaining ¾ cup breadcrumbs in a shallow dish. Shape crabmeat mixture into 4 patties. Coat patties in breadcrumbs, and place on prepared pan. Carefully cover with plastic wrap, and refrigerate 1 hour.
4. Heat a large skillet over medium heat until hot, 3 to 5 minutes. Add oil and crab cakes to skillet; cook until golden brown, 3 to 5 minutes per side. Serve immediately with New Orleans Remoulade.

THE GULF COAST BLUE CRAB INDUSTRY is largely made up of family-owned, independent commercial crabbers working their own traps from small vessels and passing down the trade through generations. Together, the Gulf Coast states of Louisiana, Florida, Texas, Alabama, and Mississippi account for about 32% of all domestic blue crab caught, averaging around 51 million pounds each year. That's enough to make more than 40 million crab cakes—about six for every person living along the Gulf Coast.

Tomato Pie

Makes 1 (9-inch) pie; 6 servings

Making a tomato pie is all about finding the ripest fruit. Only peak-season tomatoes bursting with sweetness and bright acidity can deliver. There is no solution or shortcut for making this pie taste great off-season—short of flying to the opposite hemisphere. Luckily, tomatoes are generally plentiful and abundant June through September. (Although timing varies depending on where you live.) But that's only half the story. Layered between those tomato slices is a mayonnaise-forward, cheesy filling that bakes until golden on top and set. Mayonnaise lets you skip any special tempering or the need to add flour to prevent the filling from curdling. It's creamy, with sautéed onion and fresh basil coming through to accent the tomatoes and the custardy filling. The dough for the crust comes together easily with a mix of butter and mayonnaise and turns out tender and flaky when baked.

1¾ pounds vine-ripe tomatoes, sliced crosswise ¼ inch thick and seeded
2 teaspoons kosher salt, divided
1 tablespoon vegetable oil
1 cup chopped yellow onion
Mayonnaise Piecrust (recipe follows)
2 cups shredded Monterey Jack cheese
¾ cup Blue Plate Mayonnaise
½ cup thinly sliced fresh basil
¼ teaspoon ground black pepper
1 large egg, lightly beaten
Garnish: fresh basil leaves

1. Line 2 to 3 baking sheets with paper towels. Place tomato slices on prepared pans; sprinkle with 1 teaspoon salt. Let stand at room temperature for 30 minutes; pat dry. Let stand for 30 minutes more; pat dry.
2. In a medium skillet, heat oil over medium heat. Add onion, and sauté until softened and translucent, 5 to 8 minutes. Let cool completely.
3. On a lightly floured surface, roll Mayonnaise Piecrust into a 12-inch circle. Transfer to a 9-inch pie plate. (It should be an inch larger around the pie plate once plate is lined with dough.) Fold excess dough beneath itself; crimp as desired. Prick bottom with a fork, and freeze for 15 minutes.
4. Position oven rack in bottom third of oven. Preheat oven to 425°F.
5. In a medium bowl, stir together cooled onion, cheese, mayonnaise, basil, remaining 1 teaspoon salt, pepper, and egg. Spread half of cheese mixture in bottom of prepared crust. Layer half of tomato slices in an overlapping pattern on top of cheese mixture in crust; top with remaining cheese mixture. Top with remaining tomato slices.
6. Bake until crust is golden brown and center is set, 40 minutes to 50 minutes, covering crust with foil after 20 minutes of baking to prevent excess browning. Serve warm or at room temperature, or cover and refrigerate for up to 2 days. Garnish with basil, if desired.

Mayonnaise Piecrust

Makes 1 (9-inch) pie

2 cups all-purpose flour
½ teaspoon kosher salt
⅛ teaspoon baking powder
¼ cup cold unsalted butter, cubed
¼ cup Blue Plate Mayonnaise
¼ cup ice-cold water, plus more if needed

1. In a large bowl, whisk together flour, salt, and baking powder. Add butter, and cut in with a pastry blender until mixture is crumbly and butter is pea sized. In a small bowl, whisk together mayonnaise and ¼ cup water. Pour into flour mixture. Mix with hands or a fork until a dough ball forms, adding more water, 1 teaspoon at a time, if needed. Shape dough into a disc.
2. Wrap disc of dough in heavy-duty plastic wrap and store in the refrigerator for up to 2 days or in the freezer for up to 3 months. Let frozen dough thaw in refrigerator overnight before using.

Salting the tomato slices before baking draws out excess moisture to prevent a soggy piecrust and watery filling. This process also suppresses any bitterness, producing a sweeter more intense tomato flavor. Alternating the cheese mixture and the tomatoes helps bind everything together while baking, making the pie slice easily and creating beautiful layers.

Once the cornmeal in this batter has rested to become nicely moistened, it's the right time to begin frying hush puppies. The centers steam to a tender crumb cooking in the hot oil, while the outside forms a toasty, lightly sweet crust that holds the rounded shape. Cornmeal is an essential for your pantry (page 25), so keep enough stocked when a spur-of-the-moment craving hits to serve hush puppies along with dinner. Stir up some Tartar Sauce (page 219) or your favorite dip to serve with them.

CLASSIC
HUSH PUPPIES
JALAPEÑO
AND CORN
HUSH PUPPIES
CHEDDAR
CHEESE
HUSH PUPPIES

HUSH PUPPIES 3 WAYS

Classic Hush Puppies

Makes about 21

Hush puppies have their share of origin stories, but what remains constant is the cornmeal batter dropped into hot oil, a fixture of the Gulf South fish fry for generations. Commonly on the plate alongside fried catfish and shrimp, hush puppies are the perfect bread option. The secret to this hush puppy is in the batter. Mayonnaise brings fat and acts as a binder that holds the batter together. Each hush puppy fries up with a crispy exterior that cracks open to a warm, tender crumb. Rest the batter for 10 minutes before frying: If you skip this step, the cornmeal won't fully hydrate and the interior will feel gritty.

Vegetable oil, for frying
1½ cups self-rising yellow cornmeal
¾ cup self-rising flour
1½ tablespoons granulated sugar
1 teaspoon kosher salt
¾ cup whole buttermilk, room temperature
½ cup Blue Plate Mayonnaise, room temperature
1 large egg, room temperature, lightly beaten

1. In a large Dutch oven, pour oil to a depth of 3 inches, and heat over medium-high heat until a deep-fry thermometer registers 360°.
2. In a large bowl, stir together cornmeal, flour, sugar, and salt. Add buttermilk, mayonnaise, and egg, stirring until moistened. Let stand for 10 minutes.
3. Using a 1½-tablespoon spring-loaded scoop, drop batter into hot oil in batches. Fry, turning frequently, until golden brown, 3 to 4 minutes. Let drain on a wire rack. Serve immediately.

Cheddar Cheese Hush Puppies

Prepare the classic batter, adding 8 ounces shredded sharp Cheddar cheese to the cornmeal, flour, sugar, and salt before adding the wet ingredients. Fry for 3 to 4 minutes.

Jalapeño and Corn Hush Puppies

Prepare the classic batter, then fold in 1¼ cups freshly cut corn kernels, ¼ cup grated sweet onion, and 2 seeded and finely chopped medium jalapeños after combining the wet and dry ingredients. Fry for 3 to 4 minutes. For a milder result, substitute red bell pepper for the jalapeño.

Whether planted in small courtyards, containers and pots on porches, raised beds, or more spacious plots, Gulf South cooks have a tradition of keeping year-round kitchen gardens. Growing herbs, heirloom tomatoes, peppers, okra, and greens, the home-grown produce goes straight from backyard to table.

CONTRIBUTOR

Hannah Jobe
Brand Manager,
Blue Plate Mayonnaise

New Orleans, LA

Hannah Jobe, brand manager at Blue Plate Mayonnaise, fondly recalls the splendid simplicity of her grandmother's salads. "My Granny, Bobby Jean, kept a garden full of tomatoes, onions, cucumbers, peppers, and herbs," says Jobe. "She loved having her hands in the dirt, but more than that, she loved providing for the people she cared about. It wasn't easy work, especially as she got older, but she did it year after year, because it mattered—and that only made those Granny salads all the more special."

Bobby Jean's Garden Salad

Makes 8 to 10 servings

The essence of this garden salad is simple—let whatever is popping up in the garden dictate what ends up in the salad bowl to round out the rest of the meal. There should, however, always be a few constants: homegrown tomatoes, sweet white onions, and cucumbers. Beyond that, the rest is up to you. Hannah Jobe's recipe leans into fresh corn, green bell peppers, and black-eyed peas to give the salad more earthiness and heft. When you're ready to assemble the salad, whisk the mayonnaise, vinegar, and herbs together in the salad bowl until well blended. The dressing will easily coat the vegetables, which can be added all at once and combined with a few gentle tosses. This salad is best made 30 to 45 minutes prior to eating to let all the flavors come together.

- ½ cup finely chopped fresh parsley
- ½ cup finely chopped green onion
- ¼ cup Blue Plate Mayonnaise
- ¼ cup Steen's cane vinegar or your preferred vinegar
- 1½ tablespoons finely chopped fresh oregano
- 1½ tablespoons finely chopped fresh dill
- ½ teaspoon kosher salt
- ¼ teaspoon ground black pepper
- 1 (15-ounce) can black-eyed peas, rinsed and drained
- 2 cups peeled and sliced English cucumber
- 2 cups cherry tomatoes, halved
- ¾ cup chopped sweet Vidalia onion
- ¾ cup freshly cut corn kernels (roasted, if desired)
- ½ cup chopped green bell pepper

1. Whisk together parsley, green onion, mayonnaise, vinegar, oregano, dill, salt, and black pepper in a large bowl. Add the black-eyed peas and remaining ingredients, stirring to combine. This makes about 6 cups. Let stand for 30 to 45 minutes before serving.

Mac and Cheese

Makes 10 to 16 servings

The secret to this mac and cheese is truly the mayonnaise. It takes the place of béchamel, a 4-step, roux-based French white sauce you can simply skip and still achieve a velvety smooth, creamy cheese sauce in this iconic American dish. There's no worry of the curdling or seizing that can occur when baking cheese, eggs, and cream together. Instead, mayonnaise performs as an emulsifier that binds fat and liquid together into a stable sauce that coats every noodle. Blue Plate's egg yolk-only mayonnaise contributes rich fat and subtle tang for outstanding flavor. Sharp Cheddar and melty Monterey Jack cheeses work well together to balance the dish. For a little extra heat, swap in pepper Jack for the milder Monterey Jack cheese.

- 1 **(16-ounce) package elbow macaroni**
- 2 **cups evaporated milk**
- 4 **ounces cream cheese, room temperature**
- ¾ **cup Blue Plate Mayonnaise**
- ¾ **teaspoon ground black pepper**
- ½ **teaspoon kosher salt**
- ½ **teaspoon dry mustard**
- 2½ **cups freshly shredded sharp Cheddar cheese**
- 2½ **cups freshly shredded Monterey Jack cheese**

1. Preheat oven to 350°F. Spray a 2-quart baking dish with cooking spray.
2. Cook pasta according to package directions.
3. In a large pot, whisk together milk and cream cheese, and cook over medium until melted and smooth. Stir in mayonnaise, pepper, salt, and dry mustard.
4. In a large bowl, combine Cheddar and Monterey Jack cheeses. Reserve 1½ cups, and set aside. Reduce heat to low, and gradually add remaining 3½ cups cheese mixture to sauce, stirring constantly until melted and smooth. Stir in pasta.
5. Spoon pasta mixture into prepared pan. Sprinkle reserved 1½ cups cheese mixture on top. Bake until cheese melts, about 15 minutes. Let stand 10 minutes before serving.

Creamiest Buttermilk Mashed Potatoes

Makes 6 to 8 servings

A cornerstone selection at meat-and-three spots and a regular on the dinner table at home, mashed potatoes hold a special place on Southern plates. Yukon Gold potatoes—a humble, hardworking tuber—have bold potato flavor and are the gold standard for a velvety mash. Mayonnaise, along with butter and buttermilk, brings in silky richness and the perfect amount of acidity. Butter in the cooking water helps prevent gumminess and keeps the mashed potatoes from becoming too stiff, a bonus for leftovers served the next day (see Note). Drain the potatoes well: Allowing the excess moisture to evaporate is an easy but crucial step to an extraordinary side dish.

3 pounds Yukon Gold potatoes
4 tablespoons unsalted butter, divided, plus more for garnish
½ cup Blue Plate Mayonnaise
¼ cup whole buttermilk
1 tablespoon finely chopped fresh chives, plus more for garnish
Salt and ground black pepper, to taste

1. Wash and peel potatoes; cut into quarters. Place the potatoes in a large pot of cold, salted water. Add 2 tablespoons butter, and bring to a boil. Lower heat to a simmer, and cook until potatoes are tender, about 25 minutes. Drain potatoes in a strainer, and transfer to a heatproof bowl.
2. Mash potatoes with a potato masher. (For the best texture, leave a few small chunks of potato.) Add mayonnaise, buttermilk, and remaining 2 tablespoons butter, and stir well. Stir in salt and pepper to taste.
3. Garnish with chopped chives and a pat of butter, if desired.

Note: This is a great make-ahead side dish that reheats beautifully for a big meal. Prepare a day ahead and store covered in the refrigerator. Fold in cooked, chopped bacon and shredded Cheddar cheese in step 2 for a loaded baked potato version.

Roasted Root Vegetables

Makes 4 servings

Root vegetables have a longer season than most people realize, beginning as early as late summer and running well into winter—depending on where you live—which makes this a dish worth keeping in regular rotation. Beets, parsnips, carrots, and sweet potatoes bring color, texture, sweetness, and a striking presentation as a side to a beautiful roast, a component of a charcuterie spread, or the centerpiece of a simple entrée salad. Coating the vegetables with mayonnaise helps them caramelize well and takes the place of oils. Serve with garlic or herb aioli—either will be delicious—choosing based on what else you plan to serve with the roasted vegetables. A note on cutting: uniform size matters more than uniformity of shape. And capitalize on the vegetables' natural shapes to guide you. While roasting, arrange like vegetables on the pans together, considering density and size, so you can easily pull off any smaller or quicker cooking pieces that finish first.

1 pound rainbow carrots, peeled, halved lengthwise, and cut into 2-inch pieces
1 pound sweet potatoes, cut into 3-inch pieces
2 parsnips, peeled and cut into 3-inch pieces
1 golden beet, peeled and cut into 8 wedges
1 red beet, peeled and cut into 8 wedges
2 cloves garlic, smashed
⅓ cup Blue Plate Mayonnaise
1 tablespoon fresh rosemary
1½ teaspoons kosher salt
¼ teaspoon black pepper
Garlic Aioli or Herb Aioli (page 210)
Garnish: fresh rosemary

1. Preheat oven to 400°F. Line 2 baking sheets with parchment paper.

2. In a large bowl, toss together carrots, sweet potatoes, parsnips, beets, garlic, mayonnaise, rosemary, salt, and pepper until vegetables are fully coated in mayonnaise.

3. Transfer mixture to prepared baking sheets and spread in an even layer. Bake until vegetables are golden brown and just tender, 20 to 25 minutes. Serve with Garlic Aioli or Herb Aioli. Garnish with fresh rosemary, if desired.

Photo by Ryan Hodgson-Rigsbee

Blistered Green Beans

Makes 4 servings

Blistered green beans come to the table looking like you possess special cooking know-how and a lot of time. Let everyone be fooled, because all you would have spent is about 10 minutes to make this incredibly satisfying take on an everyday vegetable. The key is a ripping hot cast-iron or carbon-steel pan and perfectly dried beans after rinsing. Deliciousness comes from thinly sliced garlic that fries in mayonnaise until crispy, followed by the beans, which sizzle in the resulting infused fat the mayonnaise creates. Resist the urge to stir too soon: That direct contact with the pan is what creates the blistery char. Choose just-picked green beans when you can for the best snap and flavor. Green beans are hardy enough to hold through most of the week once you get them home.

¼ **cup Blue Plate Mayonnaise**
3 **large cloves garlic, thinly sliced**
1 **pound fresh green beans, trimmed**
½ **cup thinly sliced shallots**
1½ **teaspoons kosher salt**
¼ **teaspoon black pepper**

1. Preheat oven to 450°F.

2. Add mayonnaise and garlic to a large ovenproof sauté pan; cook over medium heat, stirring constantly, until mayonnaise melts down to oil and garlic is golden, 6 to 8 minutes.

3. Using a slotted spoon, remove garlic from mayonnaise oil, and transfer to a heatproof container. Set aside.

4. Add green beans, shallots, salt, and pepper to mayonnaise oil in pan, tossing until beans are well coated.

5. Transfer skillet to oven, and bake until green beans are blistered and shallots are lightly golden brown, 10 to 15 minutes. Transfer to a serving plate, and sprinkle with fried garlic before serving. Serve warm.

FARMERS' MARKETS and produce stands abound in the Gulf South, from large urban hubs *(see below)* to smaller roadside stands that dot the region throughout the year.

ALABAMA

Birmingham: The Farmers' Market at Pepper Place *(established 2000)*

Mobile: Market in the Park *(established 2013)*

FLORIDA: GULF COAST

Pensacola: Palafox Market *(established 2002)*

Tampa: Fresh Market at Hyde Park Village *(established 2012)*

LOUISIANA

New Orleans: Crescent City Farmers' Market *(established 1995)*

Baton Rouge: Red Stick Farmers' Market *(established 1996)*

MISSISSIPPI

Jackson: Mississippi Farmers' Market *(established 1950s)*

TEXAS: GULF COAST

Houston: Urban Harvest Farmers' Market *(established 1994)*

Squash Casserole

Makes 6 to 8 servings

Squash casserole is as Southern as it gets. It's a dish born from abundant summer gardens that makes its way to potluck dinners and easy suppers. Yellow squash and zucchini thrive in the South's long, warm growing season, and this casserole is the answer to what to make when you have more squash than you think you can handle. Same as with mac and cheese, mayonnaise replaces the work of a béchamel, binding the squash, Cheddar and Gouda cheeses, eggs, and milk into a custardy, bubbling bake that sets up beautifully in the oven. Blanching the squash before baking releases moisture and keeps the filling from becoming watery. The kettle chip topping—a fun move that takes the place of traditional crumbled butter crackers—delivers satisfying crunch and a welcome dose of salt. (If you're a traditionalist, feel free to go with crackers instead.) Serve this casserole alongside roast chicken, fried chicken, or pork chops. A dash of hot sauce, if you're game, adds a kick of heat and vinegary zing.

2 pounds fresh squash, cut crosswise into ¼-inch-thick slices, halved
1 large yellow onion, chopped (about 1½ cups)
1 tablespoon kosher salt
3½ cups crushed kettle-cooked chips, divided
1¼ cups Blue Plate Mayonnaise
1 cup whole milk
⅓ cup unsalted butter, melted
3 large eggs, lightly beaten
½ cup freshly shredded sharp Cheddar cheese
½ cup freshly shredded smoked Gouda cheese

1. Preheat oven to 350°F. Spray a 13x9-inch baking dish with cooking spray.
2. In a large Dutch oven, combine squash, onion, salt, and cold water to cover. Bring to a boil over medium-high heat, stirring occasionally. Reduce heat to medium-low; simmer until tender, about 4 minutes. Drain.
3. Line bottom of prepared pan with 1¾ cups crushed chips.
4. In a medium bowl, whisk together mayonnaise, milk, melted butter, and eggs. Fold in squash mixture and cheeses. Spoon on top of chips in pan. Top with remaining 1¾ cups crushed chips.
5. Bake until center is set, 40 to 45 minutes. Let cool for 10 minutes.

CHAPTER 3

Two-Napkin Sandwiches

Good bread, the right spread, and fillings that speak to the food pathways, culture, and history of a place are what define an amazing sandwich. Along the Gulf Coast, sandwiches span the spectrum, from po-boy classics that build from carefully fried seafood or slow-cooked meat to quick-to-fix lunch-counter favorites and garden-inspired options like a simple tomato sandwich.

THE HISTORY OF PO-BOYS

Generosity, community, and working-class solidarity created the po-boy. Tradition and innovation made it a culinary institution. In 1929, brothers Bennie and Clovis Martin, former streetcar conductors turned French Market restaurant operators, with the help of baker John Gendusa, gave away free French bread sandwiches filled with fried potatoes, gravy, and a bit of roast beef to picket-line streetcar workers in support of their cause. The Martins had no idea their generous act of feeding their "poor boy" colleagues would launch a cultural icon.

The French bread, tinkered with along the way, became iconic in its own right with a unique, shatteringly crisp crust and pillowy soft interior that is perfectly suited for absorbing drippings and sauces including mayo. Leidenheimer Baking Company and John Gendusa Bakery, both in operation in New Orleans for more than 100 years, capitalize on Louisiana's humid climate to create those perfect loaves, making them the leading providers for the bread for po-boys.

When you order a po-boy, the question you always must answer is, "Do you want it dressed?" A dressed po-boy includes lettuce, tomato, pickles, and, of course, plenty of Blue Plate Mayonnaise. In 2024, Louisiana Lt. Governor Billy Nungesser officially proclaimed Blue Plate the Official Mayonnaise of Po-Boys. But dressed means more than just adding that refreshing, crunchy, and creamy finish—it means complete; it means doing things right, fully, properly loaded. Dressed or not, a po-boy is an iconic part of the food culture of the Gulf South.

Inside a po-boy, anything goes. That original sandwich has evolved into delicious variations. There's a roast beef and gravy version that's affectionately known as a Debris Po-Boy (page 73). Fried catfish, shrimp (page 69), and oysters often show up, individually and sometimes in combinations. And a slow-roasted pork version, Cochon de Lait Po-Boy (page 70), made its debut at the New Orleans Jazz & Heritage Festival (Jazz Fest) in 2001.

Po-boys show up everywhere in New Orleans and the Gulf South: dedicated sandwich shops, corner stores, festivals, roadside stands, and white-tablecloth restaurants alike. Beyond the region, the po-boy has found its way to faraway locales including New York, Chicago, and Los Angeles.

CONTRIBUTOR

Justin Kennedy
Parkway Bakery
and Tavern

New Orleans, LA

Justin Kennedy, general manager and head chef at Parkway Bakery and Tavern, is a devoted po-boy advocate. He joined the beloved landmark, which first opened in 1911, while still a student at the University of New Orleans. Working his way up from part-time counter help and learning the ropes from the kitchen team, Kennedy went on to lead the team at the New Orleans institution, whose history is central to the po-boy origin story. That leadership means taking full responsibility for holding up the restaurant's long and storied reputation. And Kennedy has done just that: Appearing on nationally televised food shows and earning a 2025 Michelin Guide Bib Gourmand, he is, by any measure, an unofficial New Orleans po-boy ambassador.

Fried Shrimp Po-Boy

Makes 6 servings

With an ample pile of golden fried Gulf shrimp, Justin Kennedy's po-boy is a sight to behold. Roll up your sleeves, grab the sandwich with two hands, and settle into the joy of eating this masterpiece. The shrimp, dredged in Seasoned Corn Flour that includes a hint of ground clove and lemon pepper, develop a delicate crust that doesn't compete with their sweet flavor. Soft po-boy bread is a must for showcasing those succulent shrimp layered with the creamy, tangy mayo, crisp shredded iceberg lettuce, thick vine-ripe tomato slices, and crinkle-cut dill pickles.

2 pounds fresh 40/50 peeled and deveined Louisiana white shrimp or other Gulf shrimp
5 cups vegetable oil
Seasoned Corn Flour (recipe follows)
3 (12-inch) French bread loaves (see Note)
¾ cup Blue Plate Mayonnaise
3 cups shredded iceberg lettuce
2 medium-sized vine-ripened tomatoes, sliced ¼ inch thick
15 crinkle-cut dill pickle chips
Crystal Hot Sauce, to taste

1. Place shrimp in a cold-water bath.
2. In a deep frying pan or large Dutch oven, pour oil to a depth of about 2 inches. Make sure you have plenty of room to place your shrimp. Heat oil over medium heat until a deep-fry thermometer registers 350°F.
3. Place Seasoned Corn Flour in a large bowl. Drain shrimp, and dredge in the seasoned flour. Lightly drop half of shrimp in oil, and fry 2 to 3 minutes or until golden brown. Remove with a slotted metal spoon, and let drain on paper towels. Repeat procedure with remaining shrimp.
4. Cut each bread loaf in half lengthwise, and cut each half into 2 equal portions. (If preferred, place the bread on a baking sheet, cut sides up, and cook in the oven at 350°F for 1 minute or until lightly toasted.)
5. Spread mayonnaise on cut sides of bread. Place the lettuce, tomatoes, and pickles on the top (crown) side of the bread. Place fried shrimp on the bottom side of the bread; add hot sauce to taste.

Seasoned Corn Flour

Makes about 1¾ cups

1½ cups corn flour
¼ cup all-purpose flour
1½ teaspoons salt
½ teaspoon cayenne pepper
½ teaspoon garlic powder
½ teaspoon lemon pepper
½ teaspoon granulated sugar
¼ teaspoon ground cloves

1. In a large bowl, mix all ingredients vigorously until well incorporated.

Note: Use Leidenheimer or Gendusa French bread, if you can.

Cochon de Lait Po-Boy

Makes 6 servings

If you've never been to New Orleans Jazz Fest, making this po-boy is your chance to experience some of the magic. While cochon de lait *literally translates to "suckling pig," this recipe makes things approachable. A bone-in pork butt marinates in mayonnaise spiked with Creole seasoning and smoked paprika, and then braises until pull-apart tender. For the sandwich, a simple Creolaise sauce, made with egg yolk–based Blue Plate Mayonnaise, Creole mustard, and a splash of vinegar, is drizzled over the top. A pile of creamy, crunchy coleslaw offsets the pork's richness for the perfect bite. Cue the music.*

- **1 cup Blue Plate Mayonnaise, divided**
- **1 tablespoon light brown sugar**
- **¼ cup plus 1 teaspoon Creole mustard**
- **1 teaspoon Creole seasoning**
- **¼ teaspoon smoked paprika**
- **¼ teaspoon ancho chile powder**
- **⅛ teaspoon cayenne pepper**
- **1 (6-pound) bone-in pork butt**
- **2 tablespoons vegetable oil**
- **3 cups chicken stock**
- **1 tablespoon white wine or cane vinegar**
- **2 (12-inch) French bread loaves**
- **2 cups Traditional Coleslaw (recipe follows)**

1. Combine ½ cup mayonnaise, brown sugar, 1 teaspoon mustard, Creole seasoning, paprika, chile powder, and cayenne pepper in a small bowl.
2. Place pork on a plate, and score the fat cap on the pork. Spread mayonnaise mixture evenly over the pork, and refrigerate, uncovered, overnight or up to 8 hours.
3. Heat oil in a large Dutch oven over high heat. Add pork, and sear until very well browned on all sides, 4 to 6 minutes per side. Don't be afraid to let the pork get very brown. This is where a lot of the flavor comes from. Reduce heat to low, carefully add stock, cover with lid, and cook until pork is very tender and shreds easily with a fork, 3 to 4 hours.
4. Using 2 forks, pull the pork apart into thin shreds, and mix with accumulated drippings in bottom of pot. Allow meat to cool slightly and absorb juices (see Note).
5. To make the Creolaise sauce, combine remaining ½ cup mayonnaise, remaining ¼ cup mustard, and vinegar in a small bowl.
6. Cut each bread loaf in half lengthwise, and cut each half into 3 equal portions. Pile about ⅓ cup Traditional Coleslaw on each bottom half. Top with the pulled pork, drizzle with the Creolaise sauce, and top with top halves of loaves. Serve immediately.

Note: The pork can be cooked and shredded up to 3 days in advance and refrigerated until ready to serve. If prepared in advance, heat it in a 200°F oven, covered with foil, until warm.

Traditional Coleslaw

Makes about 7 cups

- **½ cup Blue Plate Mayonnaise**
- **1 tablespoon seasoned rice wine vinegar**
- **1 teaspoon celery seeds**
- **Generous pinch granulated sugar**
- **Salt and ground black pepper, to taste**
- **7 cups shredded cabbage (½ large head)**

1. Stir together the mayonnaise, vinegar, celery seeds, sugar, and salt and pepper to taste in a large bowl until well combined.
2. Add cabbage, and toss until well coated. Taste and adjust seasoning, if needed. Cover, and refrigerate until ready to serve or up to 4 days.

Debris Po-Boy

Makes 6 servings

Saturated in its own juices after braising until fork-tender, the shredded, garlic-infused roast beef and its drippings are the main event for this decadent po-boy. Originally named for the French word for débris *(meaning "scraps" or "remnants"), it referred to bits of leftover meat that fell into the drippings during roasting. For this recipe, the beef is seared first to develop caramelized flavor, with mayonnaise helping the process along. The soft French bread is the ideal home for the tender meat and its juices, a natural sponge that sops up every drop. Taken over the top with melted provolone or fontina cheese, this fully dressed sandwich isn't for the dainty—it's a three-napkin affair.*

1 (3- to 4-pound) boneless beef chuck roast
10 cloves garlic, cut in half lengthwise
1¼ cups Blue Plate Mayonnaise, divided
2 teaspoons kosher salt
1 teaspoon ground black pepper
2 tablespoons vegetable oil
3 cups beef stock, plus more if needed
2 (12-inch) French bread loaves
6 slices fontina or provolone cheese
Thinly shredded iceberg lettuce
6 slices tomato
Louisiana-style hot sauce (optional)

1. Preheat oven to 350°F. Using the tip of a sharp paring knife, make 20 evenly spaced small cuts, about 1½ inches deep, all over roast. Insert garlic cloves as deep into the cuts as possible. Rub all sides of roast with ¼ cup mayonnaise, and season on all sides with salt and pepper.
2. Heat oil in a large Dutch oven over high heat. Add roast, and sear until it is very well browned on all sides, 4 to 6 minutes per side. Don't be afraid to let the roast get very brown. This is where a lot of the flavor comes from. Reduce heat to low, carefully add stock, and cover with lid. Transfer to oven, and cook until beef is tender and shreds easily with a fork, 2 hours 30 minutes to 3 hours.
3. Using 2 forks, pull apart beef into thin shreds, and mix with accumulated drippings in bottom of pot. Allow meat to cool slightly and absorb juices (see Note).
4. Preheat broiler.
5. Cut each bread loaf in half lengthwise, and cut each half into 3 equal portions. Spread cut sides of bread with remaining 1 cup mayonnaise.
6. Place bottom halves on a baking sheet, and top with shredded meat; drizzle with extra drippings. Top meat with cheese slices. Broil just until cheese melts, 2 to 3 minutes. Remove from oven.
7. Top with shredded lettuce and tomato slices; sprinkle with hot sauce, if desired. Top with top halves of bread. Serve immediately.

Note: The chuck roast can be cooked and shredded up to 1 week in advance and refrigerated until ready to serve. If prepared in advance, heat it in a 200°F oven, covered with foil, until warm.

The Parkway Bakery and Tavern, established in 1911, joined the original po-boy movement in support of the union workers in 1929 along with the Martin brothers. They had little idea that feeding their "poor boy" colleagues would launch an icon that's now a beloved part of the region's food culture. Blue Plate has been part of that story, but it was made official in 2024 when Louisiana Lt. Governor Billy Nungesser offically proclaimed it the Official Mayonnaise of Po-Boys.

UNITED STATES OF AMERICA

UNION JUSTICE AND CONFIDENCE

State of Louisiana

Lieutenant Governor

Billy Nungesser

WHEREAS,	THE PO-BOY SANDWICH WAS FIRST CREATED DURING THE 1929 STREETCAR STRIKE IN NEW ORLEANS, LOUISIANA; AND
WHEREAS,	THE PO-BOY HAS SINCE BECOME A SYMBOL OF THE RICH CULTURAL HERITAGE OF THE STATE OF LOUISIANA; AND
WHEREAS,	BLUE PLATE MAYONNAISE WAS FOUNDED IN 1927 IN NEW ORLEANS, LOUISIANA, BECOMING ONE OF THE FIRST COMMERCIALLY PREPARED MAYONNAISE BRANDS IN THE COUNTRY; AND
WHEREAS,	THE BLUE PLATE BRAND GOT ITS INSPIRATION FROM THE POPULAR "WILLOW WARE" PLATE, A SYMBOL OF HOME, FAMILY, TRADITION, AND THE PLEASURES OF GOOD COOKING; AND
WHEREAS,	FOR NEARLY 100 YEARS, BLUE PLATE HAS BEEN A BELOVED STAPLE OF NEW ORLEANS AND SOUTHERN CUISINE; AND
NOW, THEREFORE,	I, BILLY NUNGESSER, BY THE AUTHORITY VESTED IN ME AS LIEUTENANT GOVERNOR OF THE STATE OF LOUISIANA, DO HEREBY HONOR AND RECOGNIZE

BLUE PLATE MAYONNAISE

AS THE OFFICIAL MAYONNAISE OF PO-BOYS.

In testimony whereof, I have hereunto set my hand and caused the Seal of the State to to be affixed at the City of Baton Rouge on,
JUNE 1, 2024

Billy Nungesser

Lieutenant Governor and Commissioner,
Department of Culture, Recreation and Tourism

STATE OF LOUISIANA
UNION JUSTICE CONFIDENCE
LIEUTENANT GOVERNOR

Fried Oyster BLT

Makes 2 sandwiches

There isn't much that can improve a classic bacon, lettuce, and tomato sandwich layered on mayo-toasted brioche, but fried oysters are just the thing. A generous slather of hot sauce–spiked mayonnaise ties it all together. The seasoned cornmeal dredge, a decidedly Gulf South move, seals the oysters' tender, sea-kissed flavor inside a shattering crust. Smoky strips of crispy bacon and juicy slices of ripe red tomato are the ideal companions, each one holding its own against the briny richness of the oyster. The lettuce shouldn't be an afterthought either: Butter lettuce offers a velvety suppleness; swap in romaine if you want a clean, cool crunch.

6 slices applewood-smoked bacon
Vegetable oil, for frying
½ cup all-purpose flour
½ cup yellow cornmeal
1 teaspoon kosher salt
1 teaspoon garlic powder
1 teaspoon onion powder
¼ teaspoon cayenne pepper
12 fresh oysters, shucked and drained
¼ cup Blue Plate Mayonnaise
1 tablespoon Louisiana-style hot sauce
4 slices brioche bread, toasted
2 slices beefsteak tomato
2 leaves butter lettuce

1. In a large skillet, cook bacon over medium heat 6 to 8 minutes or until crisp. Cut in half, and set aside.

2. In a heavy-bottomed skillet, pour oil to a depth of 2 inches, and heat over medium heat until a deep-fry thermometer registers 350°F.

3. In a medium bowl, whisk together flour, cornmeal, salt, garlic powder, onion powder, and cayenne until combined. Dredge oysters in flour mixture, shaking off excess.

4. Fry oysters until golden brown, 2 to 3 minutes. Remove oysters using a slotted spoon, and let drain on paper towels.

5. In a small bowl, combine mayonnaise and hot sauce. Spread mayonnaise mixture on one side of each bread slice. Top 2 bread slices with bacon, oysters, lettuce, tomato, and remaining bread slices, mayonnaise side down. Serve immediately.

CONTRIBUTOR

Peter Nguyen
Bánh Mì Boys

New Orleans, LA

New Orleans is a place where food and cultures often collide, and Peter Nguyen, a native of the city and second-generation Vietnamese American, captures that spirit at his restaurant Bánh Mì Boys. The self-taught chef and owner serves a marriage of Vietnamese and New Orleans cuisine as a way to honor and bring wider appreciation of his Vietnamese culinary heritage. The menu reflects both worlds with choices that range from Vietnamese classics, Asian-inspired offerings, and Southern and Louisiana-influenced dishes, but bánh mì sandwiches are at the center. The original Bánh Mì Boys location in Metairie opened next door to the family's gas station, and later, Nguyen added outposts in New Orleans, Mandeville, and California.

Char Siu Rib Bánh Mì with Chili Crisp-Soy Aioli

Makes 4 sandwiches

This sandwich is built on a special baguette that's airy and light with a thin crispy crust and delicate crumb. It's a departure from its French counterpart that's worth seeking out at a Vietnamese bakery, Asian market, or specialty grocery for the full bánh mì experience. In a pinch, a light French baguette works well. The meaty baby back ribs are marinated and slow-roasted, and then lacquered with a five-spice tinged glaze made with hoisin, honey, and soy sauce. Pickled daikon radish and carrot offer a punchy element while cooling cucumber and cilantro add fresh crunch and grassy brightness. For a swath of rich heat and crunch, Nguyen created a simple aioli made with chili crisp and mayonnaise.

- ½ cup rice vinegar
- ½ cup warm water
- 2 tablespoons granulated sugar
- 1 teaspoon kosher salt
- 1 cup julienned daikon radish
- 1 cup julienned carrot
- 3 tablespoons hoisin sauce
- 2 tablespoons soy sauce
- 2 tablespoons honey
- 1 tablespoon Shaoxing wine
- 1 teaspoon Chinese five-spice powder
- 1 teaspoon sesame oil
- 1 teaspoon fresh grated ginger
- 3 cloves garlic, minced
- 2 pounds baby back ribs, cut into individual riblets
- 4 Vietnamese baguettes or 2 standard French baguettes
- Chili Crisp–Soy Aioli (page 79)
- 1 English cucumber, thinly sliced lengthwise
- 2 jalapeños, thinly sliced
- 1 bunch fresh cilantro, trimmed
- Fried shallots, for garnish

1. Whisk together rice vinegar, ½ cup warm water, sugar, and salt in a jar or small bowl, whisking until sugar and salt dissolve. Add radish and carrot; let sit at room temperature for at least 1 hour. The vegetables are ready when they taste bright and tangy and have softened slightly. Refrigerate for up to 2 weeks.

2. Whisk together hoisin, soy sauce, honey, Shaoxing wine, five-spice powder, sesame oil, ginger, and garlic in a small bowl. Place riblets in a resealable plastic bag or baking dish; coat completely with the marinade. Marinate at least 2 hours or up to 8 hours or overnight for deeper flavor.

3. Preheat oven to 325°F. Remove ribs from marinade, reserving marinade. Arrange ribs on a wire rack set over a foil-lined baking sheet. Roast for 1 hour 15 minutes, basting with reserved marinade every 30 minutes. In the last 10 minutes, increase heat to broil to caramelize and char the edges. The ribs are done when the glaze is lacquered and the meat pulls easily from the bone. Let rest for 10 minutes, and then slice meat from bones or serve as riblets.

4. Cut the baguettes in half lengthwise. Warm in a 325°F oven for 3 to 4 minutes or until crust is crisp. Spread a generous layer of Chili Crisp–Soy Aioli on cut sides of each baguette. Top the bottom half with cucumber and pork, and then pile on the pickled vegetables, jalapeños, and a generous handful of cilantro. Garnish with fried shallots, if desired. Press the top of baguette down firmly—a bánh mì should be packed tight—and cut in half.

Chili Crisp-Soy Aioli

Makes about ¾ cup

1. Whisk together ½ cup Blue Plate Mayonnaise, 2 tablespoons Lao Gan Ma Spicy Chili Crisp, 1 tablespoon soy sauce, 1 teaspoon sesame oil, 1 teaspoon rice vinegar, 1 finely grated clove garlic, and a pinch of granulated sugar. Taste and adjust the seasoning, adding more chili crisp for heat, more soy for depth, more rice vinegar for brightness. The aioli should be bold, a little spicy, and deeply savory. Refrigerate until ready to use.

Vine-ripened Creole tomatoes are prized for their unique rich, tangy flavor and juicy, meaty texture that comes from the terroir of the region's silty, sandy soil that includes mineral-rich sediment from the Mississippi River. If you don't live in Louisiana, especially St. Bernard and Plaquemines parishes in the Mississippi Delta, you're unlikely to find Creole tomatoes outside the area. If you do, and it's tomato season, take advantage of this remarkable tomato.

How To Make the Perfect Southern Tomato Sandwich

Makes 1 sandwich

The tomato sandwich is a Southern summer institution, and mayonnaise is a nonnegotiable ingredient. Its richness is the counterpoint to the tomato's acidity, and between the bread, the combo is pure genius.

1. Start with the ripest largest tomato you can find. Choose Creole, a good heirloom variety, or a garden-fresh beefsteak that will be juicy and meaty but never mealy. And select one that's large enough to cover the bread in just a few slices.
2. Slice thickly. A serrated knife does the job with ease. Place the tomato slices on a paper towel just for a moment to blot off a little but not all the juice.
3. Choose bread that's sturdy but soft. Go with a country white loaf—the kind you find in the bread aisle at the grocery. Those slices have a job: to absorb those tomato juices without falling apart. Toast the bread if you like.
4. Spread a thick layer of mayonnaise on each slice, sprinkle with salt and ground black pepper, and add the tomatoes to one slice and top with the other.
5. Eat now, possibly over the kitchen sink. Why would you wait?

Perfect Grilled Cheese

Makes 1 sandwich

Cheese is a main character in this sandwich, but how you griddle the bread is what separates the good from the exceptional. The goal: golden, toasted bread that allows the interior crumb to stay soft and the cheese to melt into gooey pulls. The solution: mayonnaise. It allows the bread to crisp up perfectly and brown evenly without burning before the cheese has a chance to catch up. That deep flavor from mayo's proteins and sugars' response to heat (called the Maillard reaction) is at work here. Mayo also lends a tangy taste that contrasts nicely against the richness of the cheese inside. And about the cheese: We go with melty ones like mozzarella, Havarti, and sharp Cheddar. But you can play around and find your favorite mix. For a note of nutty flavor, use Gruyère in place of Cheddar. And if you want a straight, classic grilled Cheddar sandwich, use a combination of sharp and mild Cheddars so they melt well.

2 tablespoons Blue Plate Mayonnaise
2 slices sourdough bread
3 ounces freshly shredded cheese or 2 to 3 slices preferred cheese (see Note)

1. Spread mayonnaise on one side of each bread slice. Place 1 bread slice, mayonnaise side down, in a nonstick skillet over medium heat. Top with freshly shredded or sliced cheese and the remaining bread slice, mayonnaise side up.
2. Cook about 3 minutes, then flip, and cook the other side until the bread is a crisp and golden brown and the cheese is melted and gooey, about 3 minutes more.

Note: Freshly shredded cheese melts faster and more evenly, provides better coverage, creates a creamier texture, and allows you to control the amount of each variety of cheese more precisely.

Classic Grilled Cheese

For an ultra-melty sandwich, use 1 ounce freshly shredded mozzarella, 1 ounce freshly shredded Havarti, and 1 ounce freshly shredded sharp Cheddar.

Elevated Grilled Cheese

For an extra-creamy version, use 1.5 ounces freshly shredded Havarti, 1 ounce freshly shredded mozzarella, and ½ ounce freshly shredded Gruyère.

From crisp-crusted po-boy loaves with airy interiors to soft and neatly square Pullman-style slices, every loaf has a purpose on Gulf South tables. Start with the right stuff, so the fillings and dressings can sing.

GOOD TO THE
LEIDENHEIMER
BAKING CO.
LAST CRUMB
Since 1896
SINCE 1896
(504) 525-1575

CONTRIBUTOR

Bo Reily
President and CEO of
Wm. B. Reily & Co., Inc.

New Orleans, LA

There is something about when dads cook for the kids that cements nostalgic memories of both the food and the connection. This is the story of Bo Reily, president and CEO of Wm. B. Reily & Co., Inc. where Blue Plate Mayonnaise is made and where five generations of the Reily family have shaped its story. Some Sundays, his father, Boatner, would make the ultimate dad sandwich for the kids—it was a rare special treat. The Griswold cast-iron pan would come out, bologna and eggs would get fried, and mayonnaise would flavor the entire affair. There was never a recipe, but the taste and experience spark a memory so strong that Bo still calls it the best sandwich he ever ate.

Fried Bologna Sandwich a.k.a. Dad's Super Sandwich

Makes 1 sandwich

Frying bologna transforms it from everyday lunch meat to a crispy-edged special treat for this spin on a childhood sandwich from Bo Reily. The bread, toasted in the drippings, further accents the meaty notes, and American cheese melts onto the bread while it crisps on the underside. For lusciousness, a fried egg is sandwiched with the meat, and mayo is spread on the bread, helping create a perfectly toasted, golden exterior and bringing a bright note to each bite. A dash of hot sauce counters the richness from the cheese, mayo, and meat.

- 2 tablespoons vegetable oil
- 1 to 2 (½-inch-thick) slices bologna
- 1 large egg
- Salt and ground black pepper, to taste
- 2 tablespoons Blue Plate Mayonnaise
- 2 slices soft white bread
- 2 slices American cheese
- Louisiana-style hot sauce (optional)

1. In a large cast-iron skillet, heat oil over low heat. Cut several slits around the edges of the bologna to prevent curling, and add bologna to one side of skillet. Crack egg into other side of skillet. Cook bologna until browned, about 2 to 3 minutes per side. Cook egg until medium-set, about 2 to 3 minutes per side. Remove bologna and egg from skillet. Sprinkle egg with salt and pepper to taste.

2. Spread mayonnaise over both sides of bread, and add bread slices to skillet. Place a slice of cheese on each bread slice; cover and cook until cheese melts and bread is toasted, 2 to 3 minutes. Add bologna and egg to one bread slice; top with hot sauce, if desired, and the other bread slice, cheese side down. Serve warm.

Chicken, tuna, and egg salad sandwiches move easily between elegant tea party and baby shower fare, beloved diner lunch counters, and a no-fuss dish that's easy to whip up at home. Mayonnaise, the binder, is the constant in each version. Aim for a ratio of 2 cups protein for every ⅓ to ½ cup mayonnaise to coat the ingredients without overwhelming them. Add mix-ins like celery for crunch, fresh herbs for brightness, relish or chowchow for punch and acidity, and mustard for depth. Beyond chicken, egg, and tuna, with the right ratios and add-ins, any protein makes a great scoopable bound salad—from crawfish to shrimp, crabmeat, and ham.

Chicken Salad Croissants

Makes 9 sliders

Starting with rotisserie chicken is a time-saver. The meat is well seasoned and pulls easily from the bones, a better way to go than chopping for the best salad texture and coating. Sweetness from chopped grapes and nutty crunch from toasted pecans elevate the salad.

- ½ cup Blue Plate Mayonnaise
- 1 tablespoon apple cider vinegar
- 2 teaspoons Dijon mustard, or to taste
- 2 cups finely shredded rotisserie chicken
- ¼ cup diced celery
- ¼ cup chopped red grapes
- 2 tablespoons chopped toasted pecans
- 2 tablespoons chopped fresh parsley
- Salt and ground black pepper, to taste
- 9 small croissants

1. In a medium bowl, whisk together mayonnaise, vinegar, and mustard until smooth. Add chicken, celery, grapes, pecans, and parsley, stirring until well coated. Season with salt and pepper to taste. Cover and refrigerate for at least 30 minutes or up to 3 days.

2. When ready to serve, divide chicken salad evenly among croissants.

Creole-Style Tuna Salad Sliders

Well-drained and flaked albacore tuna is best for soaking up the creamy mayonnaise without becoming mushy. This salad has a deliciously Southern edge with celery, sweet pickle relish, green onion, Creole seasoning, and a spicy kick with hot sauce and Creole mustard's zing.

Drain 4 (5-ounce) cans albacore tuna in water well, and flake into a medium bowl. Add ⅓ cup Blue Plate Mayonnaise, ¼ cup diced celery, 3 tablespoons sweet pickle relish, 2 tablespoons thinly sliced green onion, 1 to 2 tablespoons fresh lemon juice, 2 teaspoons Creole mustard, 1½ teaspoons Creole seasoning, 1 to 2 teaspoons Louisiana-style hot sauce, and salt and ground black pepper to taste. Divide tuna salad among 7 brioche slider buns. Serve immediately.

Egg Salad Sandwiches

Perfectly hard-cooked eggs are essential for egg salad that shines. Dice the eggs so the whites are prevalent in each bite, and fold in refreshing dill and onion-y chives for an herbal note. Radish diced into the salad adds peppery crunch, but feel free to omit if you prefer a smoother bite.

Dice 6 large hard-cooked eggs,* and add to a medium bowl. Add ⅓ cup Blue Plate Mayonnaise, 1 tablespoon fresh lemon juice, and 2 teaspoons yellow mustard, stirring until creamy. Fold in ¼ cup diced radish, 3 tablespoons chopped fresh dill, 3 tablespoons thinly sliced fresh chives, 2 tablespoons chopped fresh parsley, and salt and ground black pepper to taste. Cover and refrigerate for at least 30 minutes or up to 3 days. When ready to serve, top 4 white bread slices with egg salad and 4 white bread slices. Serve immediately.

**Best way to make hard-cooked eggs: Place the eggs gently in a deep pot of cold water. Over high heat, bring to a full rolling boil. Remove the pot from heat, and set a timer for 10 minutes for firm yolks. Prepare a large bowl of ice and water. When the timer goes off, immediately put the eggs into the ice water to cool. (Quick cooling prevents a green ring from forming around the yolks.) When the eggs are completely cool, refrigerate or peel. To peel, crack on a flat surface, and roll the egg on it; remove the shell, and rinse egg.*

CHICKEN SALAD CROISSANTS
CREOLE-STYLE TUNA SALAD SLIDERS
EGG SALAD SANDWICHES

CHAPTER 4

Don't Waste a Good Day Inside

Moving a meal to the backyard somehow feels more special even when the food is casual and approachable. Fresh-caught fish that's grilled or fried, handheld options like burgers and chicken wings, and sauces and sides that make open-air dining easy to pull off—these dishes stir up lasting memories and remind you to do it more often. And this chapter gives you all the reasons you need to take it outside.

Perfect Grilled Chicken

Makes 4 servings

Mayonnaise mixed with Creole mustard, fresh lemon juice, and fresh thyme is both the marinade and the basting sauce for these chicken breasts. The marinade ensures that the white meat won't dry out while it cooks over the direct heat of the grill, and basting with it allows the skinless, boneless breasts to develop gorgeous golden color as they cook. This grilled chicken is great served with lightly dressed salad greens topped with cherry tomatoes and sliced red onion. You can also go for a heartier side of potato salad or grilled corn.

1 cup Blue Plate Mayonnaise
¼ cup Creole mustard
2 teaspoons fresh lemon juice
2 teaspoons chopped fresh thyme
Sea salt and ground black pepper, to taste
4 boneless, skinless chicken breasts
Olive oil, for grilling

1. In a small bowl, whisk together mayonnaise, mustard, lemon juice, thyme, and salt and pepper to taste until well combined. Place ¼ cup mayonnaise mixture in a separate container; cover, and set aside in the refrigerator to use for basting. Place ½ cup mayonnaise mixture in a separate container; cover, and set aside in the refrigerator to use for serving. There will be remaining mayonnaise mixture in the bowl.

2. Brush both sides of the chicken using the remaining mayonnaise mixture; place in a resealable plastic bag or covered container, and marinate for at least 2 hours and up to overnight.

3. Preheat a grill or cast-iron grill pan to medium heat (300°F to 350°F); brush grill or grill pan with olive oil. Remove chicken from bag; discard marinade.

4. Remove reserved ¼ cup basting mayonnaise mixture from refrigerator, and use it to baste chicken while grilling. Place chicken breasts, rounded side down, on the grill, brush with mayonnaise mixture, and cook for 4 minutes. If you'd like to create crosshatch grill marks, rotate the chicken and continue to cook for 4 minutes more. Flip chicken breasts, brush with the remaining mayonnaise mixture, and continue to cook for 8 minutes more or until the chicken reaches an internal temperature of 165°F. Let rest for 5 minutes before serving. Serve the chicken with the reserved ½ cup mayonnaise mixture from the refrigerator.

Spicy Chicken Wings with Alabama-Style White BBQ Sauce

Makes 4 to 6 servings

These sweet-hot wings are dredged and then grilled for a light infusion of smoky flavor (especially if using wood or charcoal). They can also be baked in the oven, making them a great make-ahead option for outdoor gatherings. Alabama-style white barbecue sauce, a 1925 invention attributed to Big Bob Gibson and his restaurant in Decatur, Alabama, is a creamy, peppery sauce that's tangy and bright from mayonnaise and vinegar and ideal for rich wings, smoked chicken, grilled pork chops, ribs, and any other rich meats coming off the grill.

1 cup Blue Plate Mayonnaise
1 cup Louisiana-style hot sauce
¼ cup Steen's cane syrup
2 tablespoons fresh lemon juice
4 pounds chicken wings, wing tips removed, and divided at the joint
Olive oil, for grilling
2 cups all-purpose flour
1 teaspoon salt
½ teaspoon cayenne pepper
Alabama-Style White BBQ Sauce (recipe follows)

1. In a large bowl, whisk together mayonnaise, hot sauce, cane syrup, and lemon juice until smooth. Add wings to bowl, tossing until wings are completely covered in marinade. Refrigerate for at least 4 hours and up to overnight.
2. Preheat grill or a cast-iron grill pan to medium heat (300°F to 350°F). Brush clean grill grates or grill pan with olive oil. Line 2 baking sheets with aluminum foil; place wire racks in pans. Spray well with cooking spray.
3. Place flour, salt, and cayenne pepper in a large resealable bag, and shake well.
4. Transfer wings from marinade onto prepared baking sheets. Place wings, in batches, into the flour mixture, and shake well to coat. Dunk wings back into marinade, and then transfer to the prepared baking sheets. Repeat procedure until all wings are coated.
5. Place wings on grill; cover, and cook for about 4 minutes per side or until they are crisped and reach an internal temperature of 165°F. Serve immediately with Alabama-Style White BBQ Sauce or your favorite dipping sauce.

Baking Method: Preheat oven to 400°F. Line 2 baking sheets with aluminum foil; place wire racks in pans. Spray well with cooking spray. Follow Steps 3 and 4, and then bake wings for about 20 minutes or until they are slightly crisped and reach an internal temperature of 165°F.

Alabama-Style White BBQ Sauce

Makes about 1½ cups

1 cup Blue Plate Mayonnaise
¼ cup apple cider vinegar
1 teaspoon finely minced garlic, mashed to a paste
1 teaspoon finely grated onion
1 teaspoon Worcestershire sauce
½ teaspoon kosher salt
1½ teaspoons ground black pepper
¼ teaspoon Louisiana-style hot sauce

1. In a medium bowl, whisk together all ingredients. Cover and refrigerate until ready to use. The sauce can be made in advance and refrigerated in a resealable container for up 3 days.

Mayonnaise-based basting sauces form a protective coating that helps seasonings cling and promotes browning during grilling. If you plan to use the sauce for serving, reserve that portion separately to keep it food-safe.

BLUE PLATE
Real
MAYONNAISE

Grilled Ribeyes and Smashed Potatoes with Easy Bearnaise

Makes 4 servings

These marbled ribeyes get a brush of herb-seasoned mayonnaise before going on the grill. Eight minutes later, you have medium-rare steaks with a beautiful, caramelized exterior and deep meaty flavor. Baby potatoes, quickly parboiled and then smashed and grilled to add some char, complete the meal. Bearnaise, a tarragon, white wine, and butter sauce made easy with a head start from mayonnaise, gives the dish an effortless upgrade—a perfect solution for outdoor entertaining. Make sure to give the meat proper resting time both before and after grilling (before to take the chill off the steaks and after to prevent internal juices from running out when you slice).

- 1 **pound baby Yukon Gold potatoes (about 1½ inches)**
- 2 **teaspoons kosher salt, plus more to taste**
- 2 **(1-pound) boneless ribeye steaks**
- **Ground black pepper, to taste**
- 1 **cup Blue Plate Mayonnaise**
- 3 **tablespoons chopped fresh tarragon**
- ½ **teaspoon lemon zest**
- 1 **tablespoon fresh lemon juice**
- 1 **teaspoon Dijon mustard**
- 1 **teaspoon finely chopped shallot**
- ½ **teaspoon finely chopped garlic**
- 2 **tablespoons vegetable oil, for grilling**
- 2 **tablespoons unsalted butter, melted and cooled slightly**
- 1 **tablespoon dry white wine**

1. In a medium saucepan, combine potatoes and 2 teaspoons salt; add water to cover. Bring to a boil over medium-high heat. Reduce heat, and simmer until tender (a sharp knife should be easily inserted through the center), about 12 minutes. Let drain; cool slightly.
2. Coat the underside of a spatula with cooking spray, and use it to gently smash potatoes to about ½-inch thickness.
3. Remove steaks from refrigerator, and let stand 30 minutes. Pat dry with a paper towel. Season both sides with salt and pepper.
4. In a medium bowl, whisk together mayonnaise, tarragon, lemon zest, lemon juice, mustard, shallot, and garlic. Spoon ½ cup mayonnaise mixture into a small bowl to use for basting. Reserve remaining mayonnaise mixture, and refrigerate until ready to serve.
5. Preheat grill to medium-high heat (350°F to 400°F). Brush clean grill grates with vegetable oil. Brush each side of steaks with 1 tablespoon mayonnaise mixture. Grill steaks, cooking to desired doneness and internal temperature: 120°F for rare, about 3 minutes per side; 130°F for medium-rare, about 4 minutes per side; 140°F for medium, about 5 minutes per side; 150°F for medium-well, about 6 minutes per side; and 160°F or higher for well done, about 7 minutes per side. Transfer steaks to a platter, and tent with aluminum foil. Let rest for at least 5 minutes before serving.
6. Brush both sides of potatoes with remaining ¼ cup mayonnaise mixture. Place on grill rack. Cook until grill marks form, about 4 minutes per side. Season with salt and pepper to taste.
7. To make the Easy Bearnaise, whisk melted butter and wine into reserved mayonnaise mixture. Serve with steak and potatoes.

CONTRIBUTOR

Robert St. John
Founder and CEO
New South
Restaurant Group

Hattiesburg, MS

A native of Hattiesburg, Mississippi, Robert St. John opened his first restaurant, the now-closed but award-winning Purple Parrot Café, more than 30 years ago. Credited with putting Hattiesburg on the fine dining map, St. John continues to be a force in the restaurant and hospitality scene with six restaurants and two bars in his New South Restaurant Group roster, including Ed's Burger Joint, where his Mississippi Comeback Sauce is featured. With a focus on Gulf Coast cuisine and Creole and Cajun flavors, St. John wears many hats in the culinary world—restaurateur, Emmy Award–winning producer, spokesperson, and cookbook author committed to ensuring Mississippi's culinary stories and history are preserved. An active philanthropist engaged in hunger relief and other causes, St. John regularly supports food pantries, soup kitchens, and efforts for families of first responders.

Backyard Burgers with Comeback Sauce

Makes 8 burgers

This thick burger is fortified with shallot, garlic, Dijon mustard, and a touch of brown sugar for a complex flavor beyond simple ground beef. Served on a brioche bun and slathered with plenty of Robert St. John's Mississippi Comeback Sauce, this patty is juicy and flavorful. Comeback Sauce, a Jackson, Mississippi, original with Greek diner roots, is considered a state-wide point of pride, and story has it the name was coined to guarantee patrons return again and again. Think of this pinkish-orange sauce as a cross between Thousand Island and Russian dressings, a remoulade with Worcestershire sauce and a few pantry spices that make it something all its own. Burgers, fried seafood, and salads all benefit from its zesty, savory taste and creamy consistency.

- **3 pounds (80/20) ground chuck**
- **3 tablespoons finely minced shallot**
- **1½ teaspoons finely minced garlic**
- **1 tablespoon Dijon mustard**
- **1 tablespoon steakhouse seasoning, divided**
- **1 teaspoon kosher salt**
- **1 teaspoon brown sugar**
- **½ teaspoon ground black pepper**
- **Sliced tomato, to serve**
- **Pinch of salt**
- **8 brioche buns**
- **Romaine lettuce, to serve**
- **Mississippi Comeback Sauce (page 105)**

1. In a large bowl, combine ground beef, shallot, garlic, Dijon mustard, 1½ teaspoons steakhouse seasoning, salt, and brown sugar. Mix gently by hand just until combined. Do not overmix.

2. Divide into 8 (6-ounce) portions, and form into patties about ¾-inch thick. Lightly flatten and make a slight indentation in the center of each patty.

3. In a small bowl, combine remaining 1½ teaspoons steakhouse seasoning and black pepper. Lightly season each patty with the mixture.

4. Preheat a grill or a cast-iron grill pan to medium-high heat (350°F to 400°F). Cook patties, flipping once, 4 to 5 minutes per side or until internal temperature reaches 135°F to 140°F for medium doneness. Adjust time for desired doneness. Avoid extremely high heat to prevent burning the garlic and seasoning. Let rest a few minutes before assembling.

5. Lightly season tomato slices with a pinch of salt; let stand 5 minutes, then pat dry.

6. Lightly grill cut sides of brioche buns until toasted. Layer lettuce, burger patties, and tomato slices on bottom buns. Spoon or spread Mississippi Comeback Sauce over the top, and add bun tops. Serve immediately.

Mississippi Comeback Sauce

Makes 3½ cups

- 1 cup Blue Plate Mayonnaise
- ½ cup ketchup
- ½ cup chili sauce
- ½ cup cottonseed oil
- ½ cup yellow onion, grated
- 3 tablespoons fresh lemon juice
- 2 tablespoons minced garlic
- 1 tablespoon paprika
- 1 tablespoon water
- 1 tablespoon Worcestershire sauce
- 1 teaspoon kosher salt
- 1 teaspoon ground black pepper
- ½ teaspoon dry mustard

1. In the bowl of a food processor, add all ingredients. Process until smooth and well combined.

Up and down the Gulf Coast, day boats head out and return with the day's catch, and you can pick up the freshest catch right at the dock. Larger trawlers, chasing shrimp farther offshore, will stay out for weeks at a time. Between the springtime brown shrimp run, fall's white shrimp season, royal reds that peak each September, and Gulf pink shrimp that are caught in winter, Gulf shrimping is a year-round industry.

Louise

Blackened Shrimp Skewers

Makes 12 (8-inch) skewers / 4 servings

Renowned Louisiana chef Paul Prudhomme introduced the world to blackening, the culinary technique that became a sensation in the 1980s. It's never stopped being relevant to Cajun cooking and now is used in cuisines across the Gulf South. The method involves applying a blend of spices (usually Creole favorites including paprika, cayenne, garlic and onion powders, oregano, and thyme) and searing them on a piping hot pan or grill until they darken and develop deeply savory, charred flavor. Shrimp and blackening seasoning are common partners in Louisiana cooking, and here, mayonnaise serves as both a "glue" that adheres the seasoning to the shrimp and a protective barrier that keeps them plump and juicy. The fat in the mayo also allows a richly caramelized exterior to develop.

1 cup Blue Plate Mayonnaise
1 to 2 tablespoons blackening seasoning
3 tablespoons fresh lime juice
1 tablespoon honey
3 pounds fresh jumbo shrimp, peeled and deveined
Vegetable oil, for grilling

1. In a large bowl, whisk together mayonnaise, blackening seasoning, lime juice, and honey, mixing well. Add the shrimp to the mayonnaise mixture, and toss to coat.
2. Preheat a grill or a cast-iron grill pan to medium-high heat (350°F to 400°F). Brush clean grill grates or cast-iron grill pan with vegetable oil.
3. Thread 5 or 6 shrimp on wooden or metal skewers (see Note). Grill the shrimp for 2 minutes per side or until they turn opaque and grill marks are visible.

Note: If using wooden skewers, soak them in warm water 30 minutes before grilling.

Grilled Oysters

Makes 12 servings

This classic preparation is one of New Orleans' defining dishes and a real crowd-pleaser. Just as impressive at a casual cookout as they are at an elegant dinner party, these shucked oysters are briefly grilled on the half shell, topped with butter (combined with mayo to help prevent the butter from separating), garlic, and Parmesan. If you aren't a practiced oyster shucker, ask the fishmonger to open and clean them for you, and keep them on ice until it's time to grill. Serve these oysters with an ice-cold beer or chilled white wine. Don't forget to offer everyone grilled bread to catch every last drop of the rich sauce that develops as the oysters cook.

¼ cup panko (Japanese breadcrumbs)
½ cup unsalted butter, softened
¼ cup Blue Plate Mayonnaise
2 tablespoons freshly grated Parmesan cheese
2 tablespoons chopped fresh parsley
¼ teaspoon kosher salt
¼ teaspoon ground black pepper
2 cloves garlic, grated
12 fresh oysters, on the half shell
Flaky salt, to taste
Grilled bread, to serve

1. In a small skillet, spread breadcrumbs in an even layer. Cook over medium heat until lightly browned, about 8 minutes, stirring frequently.

2. In a medium bowl, beat butter with a mixer at medium speed until creamy, stopping occasionally to scrape the bowl. Gradually beat in mayonnaise. Add cheese, parsley, kosher salt, pepper, and garlic; beat just until combined.

3. Preheat a grill or a cast-iron grill pan to medium-high heat (350°F to 400°F).

4. Spoon about 1 teaspoon mayonnaise mixture onto each oyster. Sprinkle with breadcrumbs. Add oysters to grill or grill pan; cover and cook until bubbling, 8 to 10 minutes. Sprinkle with flaky salt. Serve immediately with any remaining mayonnaise mixture and grilled bread.

FROM BACKYARD OYSTER ROASTS to raw bars and fine dining rooms, oysters have been a fixture of Gulf South coastal life for centuries. The brackish shallows where freshwater rivers meet saltwater bays—stretching from Galveston Bay in Texas to Mobile Bay in Alabama to Apalachicola Bay along the Florida panhandle—create prime conditions for cultivating the distinctly creamy, mild, and briny oysters the region is known for. It produces some of the country's most celebrated oyster varieties, including Murder Point, Grand Isle, and Bon Secour.

goodcook

CONTRIBUTOR

Lucas McKinney
Executive Chef
Josephine's
Gulf Coast Tradition

Houston, TX

Lucas McKinney is the executive chef of the Michelin-recognized Josephine's Gulf Coast Tradition in Houston, Texas, where he showcases his strong connection to growing up on the Mississippi Gulf Coast. Born and raised in Ocean Springs, Mississippi, McKinney was immersed in the world of fishing camps and charter boat fishing along the coastal waters of the Gulf. His restaurant is named for his great-grandmother. He trained under top chefs, but ultimately, his background informs the food he makes. McKinney is a devoted champion of Gulf Coast sustainability and a steward of the region's culinary heritage. From Redfish on the Half Shell and Smoked Redfish Dip to Marinated Crab Fingers, Blue Crab Rice Bowls, and Shrimp Étouffée, McKinney has become one of the Gulf Coast's most dedicated culinary advocates.

Redfish on the Half Shell with Lemon Remoulade

Makes 4 to 8 servings

What began as rustic, no-frills fish camp cooking over open fire has become a bona fide cooking technique used on backyard grills and in fine dining rooms alike. Originally, recreational fishermen would rely on the tough skin and thick scales of their redfish catch to act as the barrier between the heat and the meat while it cooked. The term "half shell" not only defines the cooking method but also the presentation—the succulent fish fillet is served with its skin and scales left intact. For his version, Lucas McKinney brushes on lemony remoulade during the last few minutes of cooking for a delicious finish. Redfish has firm flesh that holds up well through the heat of cooking and a mild, slightly sweet and clean flavor. Native to the Gulf region, redfish thrives in the area's shallow coastal bays and marshes. If you are unable to get redfish, also called red drum, you can substitute striped bass or snapper for similar results.

- 2 **to 3 hickory wood chunks or a small handful of wood chips**
- 1 **redfish on the half shell (about 2 to 3 pounds, filleted, with skin and scales intact)**
- 1 **tablespoon blackening seasoning**
- 1 **teaspoon kosher salt**
- ¾ **cup Lemon Remoulade (page 207), divided**

1. Light a medium charcoal fire on one side of the grill. Let coals burn down, then add hickory wood, and allow to smolder.

2. Pat fish dry with paper towels. Season with blackening seasoning and salt. Spread 2 to 3 tablespoons Lemon Remoulade in a thin layer over the flesh of the fish.

3. Place fish, skin side down, over indirect heat (other side of the grill). Close lid, and cook for 20 to 30 minutes, until flaky.

4. Spread remaining Lemon Remoulade over the fish. Return to grill for 3 to 5 minutes, until warmed and the remoulade sets. Remove and serve with the skin, or "shell," intact.

Shucking oysters is both a skill and an art. The best of the best can clean and open an oyster in seconds. That speed and precision are coveted at fish markets and Gulf South restaurants where raw oyster bars are a fixture.

Fried Catfish with Creole Ravigote Sauce

Makes 4 servings

If you're going to do a fish fry, put this catfish and the bright, herb-packed sauce on the menu. The catfish, firm-fleshed and a cornerstone in Southern cuisine, benefits from the buttermilk-mayo marinade that tempers the fish's stronger flavor without compromising texture. Ravigote *(pronounced rah-vee-GOH), the zesty mayo-based alternative to everyday tartar sauce, is the ideal companion to the craggy, crunchy fried cornmeal crust and the moist, flaky fish. It's packed with plenty of briny bite from capers and cornichons and fresh herbiness from grassy parsley, onion-y chives, and licorice notes from tarragon.*

Creole Ravigote Sauce

1 cup Blue Plate Mayonnaise
2 teaspoons chopped capers
2 teaspoons fresh lemon juice
1½ teaspoons Creole mustard
1 teaspoon chopped cornichons
1 teaspoon chopped fresh parsley
1 teaspoon finely chopped fresh chives
1 teaspoon chopped fresh tarragon
½ teaspoon prepared horseradish
½ teaspoon Louisiana-style hot sauce

Catfish

1⅓ cups whole buttermilk, divided
3 tablespoons Blue Plate Mayonnaise
4 teaspoons Louisiana-style hot sauce, divided
1½ teaspoons Creole seasoning, divided
½ teaspoon salt, plus more for seasoning
1 pound small catfish fillets
Vegetable oil, for frying
1 cup all-purpose flour
1 cup cornmeal
1 large egg
Lemon wedges, for serving

1. Make the sauce: Whisk together all sauce ingredients in a small bowl until well blended. Refrigerate until ready to use. The sauce can be made 1 day ahead.

2. Make the catfish: Combine ⅓ cup buttermilk, mayonnaise, 2 teaspoons hot sauce, 1 teaspoon Creole seasoning, and salt in a medium shallow bowl. Add catfish, tossing to coat evenly. Marinate in refrigerator for at least 30 minutes and up to 6 hours.

3. Fill a Dutch oven or cast-iron skillet about 2 to 3 inches deep with vegetable oil, and heat over medium-high heat to 350°F. Place a wire rack over a baking sheet, and set aside.

4. Whisk together flour, cornmeal, and remaining ½ teaspoon Creole seasoning, and divide evenly between 2 shallow bowls. In a third shallow bowl, whisk together remaining 1 cup buttermilk, remaining 2 teaspoons hot sauce, and egg. Dredge fish, in batches, in one bowl of flour mixture, then the egg mixture, then in the second bowl of flour mixture.

5. Drop several fillets at a time into the hot oil; fry until golden brown, about 3 to 4 minutes, depending on thickness. Transfer fried fish to prepared baking sheet. Season with additional salt, if needed. Repeat procedure with remaining fish. Serve with lemon wedges and Creole Ravigote Sauce on the side.

SOUTHERN FISH FRIES are a regional outdoor food tradition with roots that begin with the archaeological evidence of Indigenous coastal cooking. It was vital to enslaved and later freed African Americans who fished the bayous and rivers and gathered to celebrate and feed a community with affordable and accessible protein. And during Lent, Friday fish fries were held in Catholic communities across the Gulf South. The go-alongs matter, too, and include hush puppies, soft white bread, hot sauce, potato salad, and coleslaw. From the riverbanks and fish camps to church parking lots and backyards, these fish fries are cultural institutions without walls.

Creamy Coleslaw

Makes 8 servings

Sweetness is present in this coleslaw but so is a little heat. Yellow, red, and green bell peppers join the backbone of this slaw—green cabbage—to lend underlying sweetness and juicy crunch. Mayonnaise, salt, black pepper, cayenne pepper, and ground chipotle chile powder are all the seasonings needed to balance and add a little fiery edge. A bit of orange zest and juice bring in acidity (and a light citrusy fragrance) without going sour as a lemon would. You can shred the cabbage on a grater, if you prefer thin strands, or hand-cut the head for thicker pieces.

- ½ **large head green cabbage, hand cut or shredded**
- 1 **medium red bell pepper, seeded and diced**
- 1 **medium yellow bell pepper, seeded and diced**
- 1 **medium green bell pepper, seeded and diced**
- ½ **cup Blue Plate Mayonnaise**
- 2 **tablespoons white wine vinegar**
- 1½ **teaspoons orange zest**
- 2 **tablespoons fresh orange juice**
- 1½ **teaspoons granulated sugar**
- 1 **teaspoon kosher salt**
- ¼ **teaspoon ground black pepper**
- ⅛ **teaspoon cayenne pepper**
- ⅛ **teaspoon ground chipotle chile powder (optional)**

1. In a large bowl, combine cabbage and bell peppers. Set aside.

2. In a small bowl, whisk together mayonnaise, vinegar, orange zest, orange juice, sugar, salt, black pepper, cayenne, and chipotle chile powder, if desired. Pour over cabbage mixture, and toss until well combined. Cover with plastic wrap, and refrigerate up to 1 day.

The still waters of the Gulf South's cypress swamps, with trees draped in Spanish moss, are among the region's most recognizable landscapes. Rich in wildlife, these ecosystems have long attracted anglers, hunters, and those eager to explore the remarkable flora and fauna.

Fried Green Tomato Stack with Green Goddess Dressing

Makes 4 servings

Whoever first thought to bread and fry unripe tomatoes can certainly be called a culinary genius. When the garden is full of more tomatoes than seems humanly possible to get through, this stacked salad will help deliciously manage the harvest. An egg and mayonnaise dip followed by a spiced cornmeal dredge gives these crusted tomato slices all their personality. (Don't skip salting and draining the tomatoes to ensure the crispiest results.) Serve this salad in short individual stacks, or pile it high for a family-style presentation. If needed, stake taller stacks with a skewer to keep them steady as you bring the dish to the table.

1½ pounds green tomatoes, cut into 16 (¼-inch-thick) slices
3½ teaspoons kosher salt, divided
16 slices thick-cut bacon
Vegetable oil, for frying
½ cup all-purpose flour
2 large eggs
2 tablespoons Blue Plate Mayonnaise
1 cup plain yellow stone-ground cornmeal
1 teaspoon garlic powder
1 teaspoon onion powder
1 teaspoon paprika
½ teaspoon ground black pepper
Green Goddess Dressing (page 217)

1. Line a baking sheet with several layers of paper towels; top with a wire rack. Place tomato slices on prepared rack; sprinkle tomato slices with 2 teaspoons salt. Let stand 30 minutes. Pat dry with a paper towel.
2. In a large skillet, cook bacon over medium heat 6 to 8 minutes or until crisp. Remove from skillet, cut in half, and set aside.
3. In a 12-inch cast-iron skillet, pour oil to a depth of ½ inch, and heat over medium heat until a deep-fry thermometer registers 350°F. Line a baking sheet with several layers of paper towels.
4. Place flour in a small, shallow bowl. In another small, shallow bowl, whisk together eggs and mayonnaise. In a third small, shallow bowl, stir together cornmeal, remaining 1½ teaspoons salt, garlic powder, onion powder, paprika, and pepper. Dredge tomato slices, one at a time, into flour, then egg mixture, and then in cornmeal mixture. Place dredged tomatoes on prepared wire rack over a baking sheet.
5. Working in batches, fry tomatoes until golden brown, 2 to 3 minutes per side. Using a spider strainer or a slotted spatula, remove from skillet, and drain briefly on paper towels in prepared baking sheet. Stack 4 fried tomatoes on each of 4 plates, placing halved bacon slices between the stacked tomatoes. Serve immediately with Green Goddess Dressing.

SOUTHERN POTATO SALAD
POTATO SALAD CROQUETTES
SEAFOOD BOIL POTATO SALAD

POTATO SALAD 3 WAYS

Southern Potato Salad

Makes 8 servings

Everyone's mother (or maybe grandmother or aunt) makes the best potato salad, and usually, it's something from memory that comes to be from a feeling and taste. This Southern potato salad feels like the one you grew up eating. It's creamy thanks to the rich mayonnaise, includes hard-cooked eggs, the crunch of celery and green onions, two types of mustard, and pickles (if you wish). Best of all, you can take it in almost any direction you like. With a few simple adjustments, you can borrow from the custom of cooking potatoes at a seafood boil by boiling your potatoes in the same seasonings. Or mold the chilled leftovers into balls and fry them, a recipe inspired by Louisiana blogger and recipe developer Jolie Meaux's way of pairing them with gumbo (see page 172).

2 pounds red potatoes, peeled, if desired, and cut into ½-inch cubes
1½ cups Blue Plate Mayonnaise
¼ cup chopped celery
¼ cup chopped green onion
2 tablespoons sweet pickle relish (optional)
1 tablespoon chopped fresh parsley, plus more for garnish
1 tablespoon yellow mustard
1 teaspoon Creole mustard
2 hard-cooked eggs, coarsely chopped
Salt and ground black pepper, to taste

1. Place potatoes in a large pot of cold, salted water. Bring water to a boil, reduce heat to a simmer, and cook until potatoes are tender, about 15 minutes. Drain, and set aside to cool.
2. In a large bowl, whisk together mayonnaise; celery; onion; relish, if desired; parsley; and mustards. Fold in potatoes and eggs, and stir to combine. Season with salt and pepper. Cover and chill until ready to serve. Keeps up to 3 days. When ready to serve, garnish with parsley, if desired.

Seafood Boil Potato Salad

Prepare Southern Potato Salad as directed, adding 1 tablespoon concentrated liquid crab boil to the pot when cooking the potatoes. For the mayonnaise mixture, omit the sweet pickle relish and fresh parsley and add 2 tablespoons prepared horseradish and ½ teaspoon no-salt-added Cajun seasoning before folding in the potatoes and eggs. Garnish with thinly sliced green onion in place of chopped parsley, if desired.

Potato Salad Croquettes

Line a rimmed baking sheet with parchment paper. Coarsely mash 3 cups cold leftover potato salad with a potato masher. Scoop 1½-tablespoon mounds of potato salad onto the prepared pan. Cover with plastic wrap, and freeze at least 20 minutes until firm.

Fill a medium Dutch oven halfway with neutral oil, and heat over medium-high heat to 375°F. Whisk together 1 cup flour and 1 tablespoon no-salt-added Cajun seasoning in a shallow bowl. Whisk together 2 large eggs and 2 tablespoons water in a second bowl. Place 2 cups panko (Japanese breadcrumbs) in a third bowl. Working in batches, dredge croquettes in the flour mixture, dip in the egg wash, then coat in panko. (If croquettes begin to thaw between batches, return to the freezer for 5 minutes before frying.) Fry until golden brown, 2 to 3 minutes. Drain on paper towels. Serve over gumbo or as an appetizer with a dipping sauce.

A favorite of home gardeners and local farmers alike, okra flourishes in the summer heat. Its pale yellow flowers bloom and fade very quickly. A few days later, the slender green okra are ready to pick while they're still small and tender.

Pickled Okra Salad

Makes 8 servings

Crunchy pickled okra becomes a star ingredient when cut into bite-sized pieces and served alongside pretty pink pickled red onions. Starting with store-bought pickled okra (and its brine used to quickly cure the slices of red onion) is the time-saving move that gets this salad to the table fast. Served on a bed of red leaf lettuce, the salad benefits from the creamy, punchy Cajun Ranch Dressing.

1 (16-ounce) jar pickled okra, undrained
¾ cup sliced red onion
1 head red leaf lettuce, torn
8 small tomatoes, quartered or halved
Cajun Ranch (page 216)

1. Remove 8 okra and ⅓ cup brine from jar. Cut okra into ½-inch-thick slices. In a shallow bowl, combine okra, ⅓ cup brine, and onion. Cover, and let stand for 1 hour. Drain.
2. Arrange lettuce, tomatoes, and okra mixture on a serving platter. Serve immediately with Cajun Ranch Dressing.

CHAPTER 5

Let the Good Times Roll

In the Gulf South, there is little need for a reason to entertain or plan a party. Hosts welcome guests into their homes and serve a variety of small bites, dips, spreads, and snacks to suit the occasion. Treasured classics mingle with regional favorites, from pimento cheese spread and shrimp remoulade to savory hand pies, crawfish-filled party fare, and beloved restaurant dishes adapted for home entertaining.

The Dynamic Duo: Mayonnaise and cream cheese are the foundation of countless Southern dips. They combine well for a perfect scoopability and evenly suspend add-ins like boudin or shrimp. Their differences are complementary: Cream cheese is dense with mild flavor; mayonnaise, tangy and rich, is more fluid. The combo tempers bold flavors and is endlessly adaptable as a base for a reliable party starter.

Hot Boudin Dip

Makes 6 servings

Boudin is the star of the show in this hot, cheesy dip made for easy entertaining. The fully cooked savory sausage needs only to be removed from its casing and sautéed with bell pepper to build flavor. Once cooled, the mixture is stirred together with cream cheese, mayonnaise, and Monterey Jack. Cajun spice, smoked paprika, and garlic powder add an additional layer of bold flavor. Baked until bubbling, this smoky, spicy dip is meant to be served with crackers and chips, but you may be tempted to enjoy a few forkfuls all on its own. To make this dip in advance, set it up in the baking dish you plan to serve it from, and store refrigerated until close to serving time. Let it stand at room temperature for 30 minutes before baking until hot throughout. For truly authentic flavor, consider ordering your boudin from one of the legendary purveyors in Scott, Louisiana, that will ship it to your door: The Best Stop Supermarket, Billy's Boudin and Cracklins, Don's Specialty Meats, or Kartchner's Specialty Meats.

1 pound boudin
½ cup chopped red bell pepper
1 cup freshly shredded Monterey Jack cheese with peppers
½ cup cream cheese, cubed and softened
½ cup Blue Plate Mayonnaise
⅓ cup chopped green onion, plus more for garnish
2 tablespoons all-purpose flour
½ teaspoon Cajun seasoning
½ teaspoon garlic powder
½ teaspoon smoked paprika
⅓ cup red pepper jelly
Crackers and chips, to serve

1. Preheat oven to 350°. Spray a shallow 2-quart baking dish with cooking spray.

2. Heat a medium stainless skillet coated with cooking spray over medium heat. Remove boudin from casings. Add boudin and bell pepper to skillet; cook until lightly browned, about 5 minutes, stirring and scraping bottom of skillet as needed. Let drain on paper towels.

3. In a medium bowl, stir together cooked boudin mixture, both cheeses, mayonnaise, green onion, flour, Cajun seasoning, garlic powder, and paprika until combined. Spoon into prepared baking dish, spreading evenly. Spread pepper jelly over the top.

4. Bake until bubbly, about 20 minutes. Serve with crackers and chips. Garnish with green onion, if desired.

PORK, RICE, AND CLASSIC REGIONAL SEASONINGS make up the main ingredients in boudin (pronounced BOO-dan), a beloved sausage brought to Louisiana by the Acadians, who adapted their Old-World sausage-making methods to local ingredients. The savory sausage also reflects the tradition of the boucherie, a community hog butchering event where families and neighbors gathered to make use of every part of the animal. Today, boudin remains a point of regional pride, and you're just as likely to find it in a small-town grocery store as you are in a large meat market.

Spicy Pimento Cheese Spread

Makes 2 cups

As ubiquitous as front porches, sweet tea, and college football Saturdays, pimento cheese is a Southern institution. Even if you have an off-the-shelf favorite or an heirloom recipe, you'll want to make room for this version in your party food repertoire. Heat from two sources, Cajun seasoning and Monterey Jack cheese with peppers (that's also paired with extra-sharp Cheddar), lends a welcome kick. Mayonnaise and cream cheese provide the cooling lusciousness that delivers a contrast to the heat and makes this spread one of the first things guests reach for at any gathering.

½ cup Blue Plate Mayonnaise
2 ounces cream cheese, softened
1 tablespoon apple cider vinegar
½ teaspoon Cajun seasoning
½ teaspoon smoked paprika
¼ teaspoon garlic powder
1 cup freshly shredded extra-sharp Cheddar cheese
1 cup freshly shredded Monterey Jack cheese with peppers
1 (4-ounce) jar diced pimentos, drained
2 tablespoons finely chopped green onion, plus more for garnish
Assorted fresh vegetable dippers and crackers, to serve

1. In a large bowl, beat mayonnaise and cream cheese with a mixer at medium speed until mostly smooth, about 2 minutes, stopping to scrape down sides of bowl. (Some small lumps are fine.) Beat in vinegar, Cajun seasoning, paprika, and garlic powder.

2. Stir in cheeses, pimentos, and green onion. Serve immediately with fresh vegetables and crackers, or cover and refrigerate for up to 1 week. Garnish with green onion, if desired.

Smoked Catfish Dip

Makes 4 to 6 servings

Lemon and dill bring fresh sophistication to this applewood-infused fish dip. The mild, sweet flavor of catfish leaves room for the smoke, herbs, and citrus to come through while holding its own against the creamy richness of the mayonnaise and cream cheese base. Brushed with seasoned mayonnaise and baked until golden and crisp, everyday saltines transform to a charming stage for heaping spoonfuls of the smoky spread. While salmon or trout spreads often get top billing at cocktail parties, this Gulf South take with smoked catfish can be the unique twist at yours.

¾ cup applewood chips (4 ounces)
1½ teaspoons lemon zest
¾ teaspoon kosher salt, divided
½ teaspoon ground black pepper, divided
1 (12-ounce) catfish fillet, skinned
1 (8-ounce) package cream cheese, softened
⅓ cup Blue Plate Mayonnaise
3 tablespoons fresh lemon juice
2 tablespoons chopped fresh dill
2 tablespoons chopped fresh parsley
Baked Seasoned Saltine Crackers (recipe follows), to serve
Garnish: chopped fresh dill, lemon zest, lemon wedges

1. In a large bowl, place wood chips and water to cover. Let soak for at least 30 minutes. Drain well. Place wood chips in an even layer in a roasting pan. Top with a wire rack; spray with cooking spray.

2. In a small bowl, whisk together lemon zest, ¼ teaspoon salt, and ¼ teaspoon pepper. Sprinkle fish with zest mixture, and place on prepared rack.

3. Place center of roasting pan over a large burner on the stovetop; heat over high heat until chips begin to smoke. Cover tightly with foil; reduce heat to low, and cook 30 minutes. Turn off heat, and let cool 30 minutes. Using 2 forks, shred catfish.

4. In a medium bowl, combine smoked catfish, cream cheese, mayonnaise, lemon juice, dill, parsley, remaining ½ teaspoon salt, and remaining ¼ teaspoon pepper. Serve immediately with crackers or cover and refrigerate until ready to serve. Garnish with dill, lemon zest, and lemon wedges, if desired.

Baked Seasoned Saltine Crackers

Makes 4 to 6 servings

¼ cup Blue Plate Mayonnaise
½ teaspoon garlic powder
½ teaspoon ground black pepper
¼ teaspoon paprika
⅛ teaspoon cayenne pepper
1 sleeve saltine crackers

1. Preheat oven to 350°F. Line a large rimmed baking sheet with parchment paper.

2. In a small bowl, whisk together mayonnaise, garlic powder, black pepper, paprika, and cayenne until well combined. Using a pastry brush, brush both sides of crackers with mayonnaise mixture, and place on prepared pan.

3. Bake until golden brown, 10 to 15 minutes. Let cool completely.

CONTRIBUTOR

Emeril Lagasse
Emeril's,
Emeril's Delmonico,
and NOLA restaurant

New Orleans, LA

With professional culinary school study and experience cooking in restaurants in Paris and Lyon, France, Emeril Lagasse arrived in New Orleans to run the kitchen at Commander's Palace before branching out on his own to open Emeril's, Emeril's Delmonico, and NOLA restaurant. From that New Orleans base, he built a national restaurant empire, opening more than 20 restaurants in cities around the United States.

Lagasse developed a style rooted in elevated and innovative interpretations of Creole and Cajun cooking influenced by his Portuguese heritage with its strong traditions of fresh seafood, bold flavors, and family-centered meals. His enthusiasm for the cuisine and its dynamic flavors launched him onto the national stage through appearances on Food Network and ABC's *Good Morning America*, where his catchphrases "Bam!" and "Kick It Up a Notch!" made him a household name. His signature seasoning blends can be found on grocery store shelves across the country. Today, Lagasse remains one of the most influential ambassadors of New Orleans cuisine.

Crabmeat Remick

Makes 6 (6-ounce) ramekins or 9 toasts

New York may have invented Crabmeat Remick, but New Orleans, with its plentiful supply of sweet Gulf Coast blue crab, made it a treasured classic. Arriving in the 1920s by way of the Plaza Hotel to the legendary Caribbean Room, where the dish remained a signature on the menu for decades, Crabmeat Remick became a standard of white-tablecloth dining throughout the city. Emeril Lagasse has long carried the torch for this New Orleans classic, serving it at Emeril's Delmonico and helping introduce it to a new generation of diners. This is a dish that truly gets the party started. The secret is in the sauce—built on tangy chili sauce, savory seasonings, and mayonnaise to complement the sweet blue crab. Serve it at a smaller cocktail party where guests can take a seat and dig in.

1½ cups Blue Plate Mayonnaise
½ cup chili sauce (see Note)
¼ cup chopped fresh tarragon
3 tablespoons tarragon vinegar or white wine vinegar
3 tablespoons Worcestershire sauce
1 tablespoon Tabasco hot sauce
2 teaspoons celery salt
2 teaspoons minced garlic
2 teaspoons Dijon mustard
½ bunch green onions, thinly sliced
1 pound fresh jumbo lump crabmeat, picked free of shells and cartilage
1 (12-inch) French bread loaf or crostini, for serving
¼ cup freshly grated Parmesan cheese
Garnish: 5 slices bacon, cooked crisp and gently crumbled

1. Preheat oven to 400°F.
2. Whisk together mayonnaise, chili sauce, tarragon, vinegar, Worcestershire sauce, hot sauce, celery salt, garlic, Dijon mustard, and green onions in a large bowl until well combined.
3. Gently fold the crabmeat into the Remick mayonnaise. The crabmeat mixture can be made up to 3 or 4 hours in advance and refrigerated, if desired.
4. To make toasts, slice French bread into ½-inch-thick rounds; top with a mound of the Remick mixture and a sprinkling of Parmesan cheese. Bake for 8 to 10 minutes until the bread is toasted and the Crabmeat Remick is golden brown. Take care not to overcook or the mayonnaise mixture will break. Garnish with crumbled bacon, if desired.
5. Alternatively, spoon the Remick mixture into 6 (6-ounce) ramekins or brûlée dishes, and sprinkle evenly with Parmesan cheese. Bake at 400°F just until crabmeat mixture is warmed through and lightly golden on top, about 10 to 13 minutes. Serve with crostini. Garnish with bacon, if desired.

Note: This chili sauce is not a spicy sriracha type, but the classic, less sweet first cousin of ketchup, found in supermarkets near the ketchup.

Gulf Coast Shrimp Dip

Makes about 2 cups

If you show up to a party (or throw one yourself) in the Gulf South, expect to encounter shrimp in some form or another. Here, sautéed shrimp are combined with a buttermilk and mayonnaise mixture blended with roasted red peppers, green onions, lemon, and just the right amount of spicy heat. The result is a pretty, coral-colored dip that works with every season and almost any occasion. Serve it with crunchy fresh vegetables as dippers during the warmer months and buttery, toasted bread as a heartier accompaniment when the cold weather hits.

1 tablespoon unsalted butter
1½ pounds fresh medium shrimp, peeled and deveined
¼ cup chopped yellow onion
2 teaspoons minced garlic
1½ teaspoons salt, divided
8 ounces cream cheese, softened
1 cup Blue Plate Mayonnaise
½ cup chopped roasted red peppers, patted dry
2 tablespoons whole buttermilk
2 tablespoons minced green onion
½ teaspoon lemon zest
1 tablespoon fresh lemon juice
2 teaspoons Louisiana-style hot sauce
2 teaspoons Worcestershire sauce
1 teaspoon cayenne pepper
Toasted baguette slices or crackers, to serve
Assorted fresh vegetable dippers, to serve
Garnish: sliced green onion, lemon zest

1. In a medium sauté pan, melt butter over medium-high heat. Add shrimp, and cook for 1 to 2 minutes. Add onion, garlic, and ½ teaspoon salt; continue to cook until shrimp are cooked through and vegetables are tender, about 2 to 3 minutes. Remove from heat, and allow to cool slightly.
2. In the work bowl of a food processor, combine cream cheese, mayonnaise, roasted red peppers, buttermilk, green onion, lemon zest, lemon juice, hot sauce, Worcestershire sauce, remaining 1 teaspoon salt, and cayenne; pulse for about 30 seconds.
3. Add cooled shrimp mixture to the food processor. Process for 15 to 30 seconds or until just combined—the dip should be fairly chunky. Serve immediately with toasted baguette slices, crackers, or fresh vegetable dippers, or cover and refrigerate until ready to serve. Garnish with green onion and lemon zest, if desired.

Tailgate culture runs deep throughout the South, and in the Gulf South, you'll encounter regional favorites alongside classic American football fare like burgers and hot dogs. Seafood, pulled pork, deviled eggs, smoked ribs, and more are all fair game. It's an informal gathering where anyone who comes by might join the fan-fueled party. Sharing the food is the whole point.

LSU

DEVILED EGGS 3 WAYS

Classic Deviled Eggs

Makes 12

Balance is the key to this versatile deviled egg recipe. The ratio of mayonnaise to egg yolks delivers a creamy consistency that is wonderful with the classic flavorings of sweet relish, mustard, salt, and pepper. The distinctive add-ins give the two variations character and flair all their own.

6 large eggs
4½ tablespoons Blue Plate Mayonnaise
1 teaspoon sweet pickle relish
½ teaspoon yellow mustard
¼ teaspoon salt
⅛ teaspoon ground black pepper
Garnish: chopped fresh parsley, smoked paprika

1. Place eggs gently in a deep pot of cold water. Bring to a full rolling boil over high heat. Remove pot from heat, and set a timer for 10 minutes for firm yolks.
2. Prepare a large bowl of ice and water. When the timer goes off, immediately transfer the eggs into the ice water to cool. Quick cooling prevents a green ring around the yolks. When eggs are completely cool, refrigerate or peel. To peel, crack on a flat surface, and roll the egg on it; remove shell, and rinse.
3. Slice eggs in half lengthwise, and carefully remove the yolks to a small bowl. Put the whites on a serving platter or egg plate.
4. Mash yolks with a fork. Add mayonnaise, relish, mustard, salt, and pepper; stir well.
5. Using two small spoons, spoon egg yolk mixture into egg whites. Alternatively, use a spatula to transfer mixture into a plastic sandwich bag, and, using kitchen shears, snip away about ¾ inch of one corner. Gently squeeze egg yolk mixture into the egg whites. Scrape or squeeze mixture down towards the opening as you work.
6. Chill 15 minutes or up to 1 hour, uncovered, before serving. For longer storage, cover loosely with foil, leaving plenty of room at the top so the eggs are not smashed. Garnish eggs with parsley and paprika, if desired.

Muffuletta Deviled Eggs

Prepare the eggs as directed. Combine yolks, 4½ tablespoons mayonnaise, 2 tablespoons finely chopped olive salad, 2 tablespoons finely chopped assorted cold cuts, ½ teaspoon yellow mustard, ½ teaspoon fresh lemon juice, and ½ teaspoon Louisiana-style hot sauce; stir until smooth. Fill whites, and chill before serving. Garnish with finely chopped olive salad, if desired.

Chicken Cracklin' Deviled Eggs

Preheat oven to 375°F. Remove 6 large pieces chicken skin from 6 large chicken thighs, and pat dry with a paper towel. Place chicken skins in a single layer on a parchment-lined baking sheet, and bake at 375°F until golden and crisp, flipping halfway through, 16 to 20 minutes. Transfer the skins to a wire rack; sprinkle with 1 teaspoon no-salt-added Creole seasoning and ⅛ teaspoon cayenne pepper, and let cool on wire rack. Chop cracklin's to desired size. (Cracklin's can be prepared up to 2 days ahead, and stored in an airtight container in the refrigerator. Bring to room temperature or recrisp briefly in a low heat oven before using.) Prepare eggs as directed. Combine yolks, 4½ tablespoons mayonnaise, ½ teaspoon Creole mustard, ½ teaspoon no-salt-added Creole seasoning, and, if desired, ⅛ teaspoon cayenne pepper; stir until smooth. Fill whites. Top eggs with chicken cracklin's just before serving.

CHICKEN CRACKLIN' DEVILED EGGS
CLASSIC DEVILED EGGS
MUFFULETTA DEVILED EGGS

Crab Beignets

Makes 12 servings

These delightful bites feature fresh crabmeat tossed with chives, lemon zest, and a hint of garlic that's bound together with mayonnaise. Rolled and coated in a light beer batter, they are fried until puffy with an inviting golden-brown crust. This savory take on New Orleans' most famous sweet pastry makes a fun addition to any cocktail party. These beignets are best served hot, so plan your frying for after guests have arrived, and serve them right away. The crab filling can be prepared and chilled up to four hours ahead, making it easier to time the frying and serving.

- **8 ounces fresh jumbo lump crabmeat, picked free of shells**
- **⅓ cup Blue Plate Mayonnaise**
- **1 tablespoon finely chopped fresh chives, plus more for garnish**
- **1 tablespoon finely chopped shallot**
- **1 teaspoon minced garlic**
- **1 teaspoon kosher salt, divided, plus more for seasoning**
- **½ teaspoon lemon zest**
- **Vegetable oil, for frying (about 4 cups)**
- **1 cup all-purpose flour**
- **⅓ cup cornstarch**
- **1 tablespoon baking powder**
- **1 cup amber lager**
- **Classic Louisiana Remoulade (page 206)**

1. In a medium bowl, gently fold together crabmeat, mayonnaise, chives, shallot, garlic, ½ teaspoon salt, and lemon zest to combine. Set aside. Crab mixture can be made up to 4 hours ahead; keep covered and chilled.

2. In a large saucepan, pour oil to a depth of 6 inches. Heat oil over medium-high heat until a deep-fry thermometer registers 375°F.

3. In a large bowl, whisk together flour, cornstarch, baking powder, and remaining ½ teaspoon salt. Gradually whisk in beer just until blended (batter will be thick).

4. Working in batches of about 4, measure 1 heaping tablespoon of crab mixture per beignet, roll into a ball, and drop into the batter. Using a fork, toss to coat; lift the beignet from the batter, letting excess drip back into bowl. Carefully lower beignet into the hot oil. Fry, turning occasionally, until crisp and deep golden brown, about 4 minutes, returning oil to 375°F between batches.

5. Transfer beignets to a paper towel–lined plate, and season with salt. Serve immediately with Classic Louisiana Remoulade. Garnish with chives, if desired.

Braided Crawfish Bread

Makes 6 to 8 servings

At the New Orleans Jazz & Heritage Festival (Jazz Fest), folks line up for crawfish bread—a rich, creamy, cheesy crawfish filling stuffed into French bread and served hot. This recipe transforms that festival favorite into an entertaining-friendly format. A creamy crawfish filling flavored with the Holy Trinity (see page 25), Creole mustard, cheese, and mayonnaise is braided inside bread dough and baked until golden brown. The resulting loaf is easy to slice and share, making it ideal for a cocktail party or buffet table. This dish is a great nod to one of New Orleans' most beloved food traditions and a perfect way to recreate those memories at home with friends.

2 tablespoons unsalted butter
½ cup finely chopped onion
½ cup finely chopped celery
½ cup finely chopped green bell pepper
1½ tablespoons minced garlic
1 pound cooked Louisiana crawfish tails (with any fat)
1 teaspoon Worcestershire sauce
½ teaspoon Louisiana-style hot sauce
½ teaspoon kosher salt
¼ teaspoon cayenne pepper
¼ cup chopped green onion
1 cup freshly shredded provolone or mozzarella cheese
½ cup Blue Plate Mayonnaise
1 teaspoon Creole mustard
1 (1-pound) loaf frozen white bread dough, thawed according to package instructions
1 large egg
1 tablespoon water
Sesame seeds, for topping
Flaky sea salt, for topping

1. In a large skillet, melt butter over medium heat. Add onion, celery, and bell pepper; cook, stirring occasionally, until vegetables have softened, about 5 minutes. Add garlic; sauté 2 minutes.

2. Add crawfish tails, Worcestershire, hot sauce, kosher salt, and cayenne pepper; sauté until crawfish tails have warmed through and any released liquid has evaporated, about 3 minutes. Stir in green onion, and let cool.

3. Once filling is cool, stir in cheese, mayonnaise, and mustard until well combined.

4. Turn dough out onto a lightly floured surface. Roll into a 15x11-inch oval, and then transfer to a piece of parchment paper sized to fit a baking sheet. Using a small knife or bench scraper, score a rectangle on the dough, leaving 1½ inches at the top and bottom and 3 inches on either side, making sure not to cut all the way through.

5. Spread crawfish mixture in the marked rectangle. Score and cut 1-inch-wide strips down each side of the filling. At each end, trim the dough to the width of the filling. Fold each end over the filling. Starting on the left side, stretch, and fold 1 strip over the filling, ending just below the opposite strip. Continue with the same pattern on the right side, alternating, until the end. Tuck and pinch the last strip. (If dough is not sticking, dab a little water on the dough to help it seal.) Using the parchment paper, transfer to a baking sheet. Cover and let rise in a warm, draft-free place (75°F) until puffed, about 1 hour.

6. Preheat oven to 350°F. In a small bowl, whisk together egg and 1 tablespoon water; brush onto the top and sides of the braided loaf. Sprinkle top with sesame seeds and sea salt. Bake until golden brown and an instant-read thermometer registers 190°F, about 30 minutes. Let cool on pan for 10 minutes. Serve warm or at room temperature.

Nearly every po-boy imaginable and great music are the hallmarks of the Oak Street Po-Boy Festival, an annual event that takes place in the New Orleans Carrollton neighborhood. The historic street, lined with shops and music venues, fills with festivalgoers who sample everything from classic cochon de lait and shrimp po-boys to innovative twists like Voodoo Fish and Chips or escargot.

Photo by Ryan Hodgson-Rigsbee

Photo by Ryan Hodgson-Rigsbee

Shrimp Remoulade

Makes 3 to 4 servings

Of course, the shrimp are the centerpiece, but the remoulade is the foundation that makes all the difference, bringing richness, tang, and complexity to every bite. Gently poached with lemon and bay leaves to preserve their sweetness and tenderness, the shrimp contribute a delicate briny flavor that pairs beautifully with the sauce. You can make this dish with Classic Louisiana Remoulade or try it with one of the recipes starting on page 206.

8 cups water
2 lemons, sliced
4 dried bay leaves
2 pounds fresh medium shrimp, peeled and deveined
Classic Louisiana Remoulade (page 206)
Fresh salad greens, to serve
Garnish: chopped fresh tarragon

1. In a large Dutch oven, heat 8 cups water, lemon slices, and bay leaves over medium-high heat until simmering. Add shrimp; cook until bright pink and firm, about 3 to 4 minutes. Remove with a slotted spoon, and place in an ice-water bath until cool. Drain the shrimp well.
2. In a large bowl, stir together shrimp and Classic Louisiana Remoulade until coated. Serve over fresh salad greens. Garnish with tarragon, if desired.

Natchitoches Meat Pies

Makes about 24

If you travel to Natchitoches (pronounced NACK-uh-tish), the oldest settlement in the Louisiana Purchase territory, you'll find no shortage of shops and restaurants offering the town's namesake meat pies. These flaky pastry turnovers are packed with a savory mixture of pork and beef browned with celery, bell pepper, and onion and seasoned with oregano. While the meat pies are often fried, these are baked—a great move for party fare. Mayonnaise takes the place of an egg wash and encourages the pastry to develop a burnished sheen. You can form the hand pies up to a day ahead, and bake them just before serving.

1 tablespoon vegetable oil
¾ pound ground beef
¾ pound ground pork
⅔ cup minced yellow onion
½ cup finely chopped red bell pepper
½ cup finely chopped celery
3 cloves garlic, minced
2 tablespoons all-purpose flour
1½ teaspoons dried oregano
1 teaspoon kosher salt
½ teaspoon crushed red pepper
¼ teaspoon ground black pepper
Meat Pie Dough (recipe follows)
6 tablespoons Blue Plate Mayonnaise

1. In a small Dutch oven, heat oil over medium heat. Add beef, pork, onion, bell pepper, celery, and garlic. Cook, stirring frequently, until meat is browned and crumbly, about 8 minutes. Drain all but 2 tablespoons drippings. Sprinkle with flour, oregano, salt, crushed red pepper, and black pepper, and stir to combine. Let cool completely.

2. Line 2 large rimmed baking sheets with parchment paper.

3. Working with one portion at a time, roll out Meat Pie Dough on a lightly floured surface. Using a 4½-inch round cutter dipped in flour, cut rounds from dough, rerolling dough scraps once. Place dough rounds on a prepared baking sheet. Cover and refrigerate until ready to use. Repeat with remaining Meat Pie Dough.

4. Preheat oven to 375°F. Lightly brush edges of dough rounds with mayonnaise. Place 2 tablespoons filling on lower half of each round. Fold dough over filling, and press to seal. Using a fork dipped in flour, crimp along edges. Freeze pies 10 minutes.

5. Lightly brush tops of pies with mayonnaise. Bake until golden brown, 25 to 30 minutes. Serve warm.

Meat Pie Dough

Makes 2 portions

5¾ cups all-purpose flour
1 tablespoon kosher salt
1¼ teaspoons baking powder
¾ cup lard or all-vegetable shortening
1½ cups whole milk
2 large eggs

1. In a large bowl, whisk together flour, salt, and baking powder. Using a pastry blender or 2 forks, cut in lard until mixture is crumbly.

2. In a small bowl, whisk together milk and eggs. Pour egg mixture over flour mixture, and stir until a dough starts to form. Knead together 3 to 4 times, and let rest for 10 minutes.

3. Divide dough in half. Wrap each half in plastic wrap. Refrigerate at least 1 hour or up to overnight before using.

Cheese Coins

Makes about 40

Essentially cheese straws in a different shape, these coin-shaped crackers share the same rich Cheddar flavor and long history on Southern cocktail tables. A thoughtful hostess gift to bring to a holiday cocktail party, cheese coins are also wonderful to serve at bridge clubs, baby and bridal showers, and more. They pair nicely with iced tea, complement the nutty notes of a chilled dry sherry, and bring out caramel and vanilla flavors in bourbon. The dough comes together in the food processor, and the slice-and-bake method makes forming uniformly sized crackers practically foolproof.

2 cups all-purpose flour
2 cups freshly shredded sharp Cheddar cheese, room temperature
6 tablespoons Blue Plate Mayonnaise
6 tablespoons cold unsalted butter, cubed
½ teaspoon kosher salt
¼ teaspoon garlic powder
¼ teaspoon paprika
¼ cup whole milk
Garnish: smoked paprika, cayenne pepper

1. Preheat oven to 350°F.
2. In the work bowl of a food processor, pulse flour, cheese, mayonnaise, butter, salt, garlic powder, and paprika until combined. With processor running, add milk until a soft dough forms.
3. Roll dough into a 1½-inch-wide log. Wrap in plastic wrap, and freeze until firm, 20 to 30 minutes.
4. Unwrap dough, and cut into ¼-inch-thick slices. Using a metal spatula, gently lift and place ¾ inch apart on 3 ungreased large rimmed baking sheets.
5. Bake until golden brown and crisp, 18 to 22 minutes. Garnish with smoked paprika and cayenne, if desired.

Mississippi Delta Hot Tamales

Makes 24

Emerging from Mexican tamale traditions and shaped by African American foodways and Southern cooking, Mississippi Delta hot tamales became staples of cafés, roadside stands, and juke joints throughout the region. These tamales, inspired by the Mississippi Delta version, use chili powder to flavor the masa and season the pork shoulder, which slowly roasts until pull-apart tender. The savory filling is wrapped in corn husks, then the tamales are gently simmered in a seasoned broth and served with saltine crackers and hot sauce. Today, tamales are as much a part of the region's culture as barbecue, catfish, and the Delta-born blues itself.

2¼ pounds boneless pork shoulder, trimmed
½ cup Blue Plate Mayonnaise
2¼ teaspoons kosher salt, divided
2 teaspoons garlic powder, divided
½ teaspoon ground black pepper
½ teaspoon paprika
2 quarts plus 3¼ cups warm chicken or beef broth, divided (plus more, if needed)
1 (8-ounce) can tomato sauce
2½ tablespoons chili powder, divided
4 cups instant masa flour
2 teaspoons baking powder
1 cup all-vegetable shortening
1 teaspoon ground cumin
24 dried corn husks, soaked in hot water until softened
Saltine crackers and Louisiana-style hot sauce, to serve

1. Preheat oven to 300°F. Line a 13x9-inch baking pan with foil.

2. Using a sharp knife, make several ¼-inch-deep cuts on both sides of pork. In a small bowl, whisk together mayonnaise, ¼ teaspoon salt, ½ teaspoon garlic powder, pepper, and paprika. Brush pork all over with mayonnaise mixture. Place on prepared pan.

3. Bake until tender throughout, 2 hours 30 minutes to 3 hours, loosely covering with foil during the last 30 minutes. Let pork cool slightly; coarsely chop. Set aside 3 tablespoons pan drippings and 4¼ cups chopped pork. Reserve any remaining pork for another use.

4. In a narrow stockpot, bring 2 quarts broth, tomato sauce, 1½ tablespoons chili powder, ½ teaspoon salt, and 1 teaspoon garlic powder to a boil over medium heat. Cover and remove from heat.

5. In a large bowl, whisk together masa flour, baking powder, 1½ teaspoons chili powder, and remaining 1½ teaspoons salt. Using fingers or a pastry blender, blend in shortening until mixture is crumbly. Gradually stir in 3 cups plain warm broth, and knead mixture in bowl with a spatula until moist and incorporated; cover with plastic wrap.

6. In a large skillet, stir together pan drippings, pork, cumin, remaining ½ teaspoon garlic powder, remaining ¼ cup plain warm broth, and remaining 1½ teaspoons chili powder. Cook over medium heat, stirring occasionally, until heated through, about 5 minutes.

7. Drain corn husks, and pat dry. Cover husks with a damp towel. Working with one husk at a time, spread about 3 tablespoons masa dough onto widest half of husk, leaving a border around edges (about a 3½-inch rectangle). Spoon about 2 tablespoons pork mixture down center of dough. Fold sides of husk over pork, allowing dough to peel from husk; press dough together, covering pork. Roll into a log. Fold narrow end of husk over seam, and secure with a strip of softened corn husk or kitchen string. Repeat with remaining masa dough, filling, and husks.

8. Stand tamales vertically, open end up, in tomato sauce mixture. Bring mixture to a gentle boil over medium-high heat; reduce heat to medium-low. Cover tops of tamales with additional corn husks (2 to 3 husks). Cover and simmer until dough is firm and pulls away from the husk, about 1 hour, adding more broth or water as needed to prevent tamales from drying out. (Do not pour liquid over tamales. Adjust heat as necessary to ensure liquid stays at a gentle simmer; do not fully boil.)

9. Remove from heat. Using tongs, remove tamales from pot, and let drain upright in a colander. Let stand about 5 minutes before serving. Drizzle with some cooking liquid, if desired. Serve with saltine crackers and hot sauce.

Blues, jazz, zydeco, Cajun, rock and roll: No matter the genre, music draws people together throughout the Gulf South. Festival International de Louisiane in Lafayette (pictured) brings Cajun and Creole music, zydeco, and sounds from France, Africa, and the Caribbean to the streets each spring. Mississippi's Delta Blues and Heritage Festival in Greenville, and the more intimate Juke Joint Festival in Clarksdale, celebrate the Delta's deep blues legacy. Springtime in New Orleans features the Jazz & Heritage Festival, a celebrated music, food, and community event.

Oven-Crisped Okra with Smoky Mayonnaise

Makes 4 servings

Okra and mayonnaise are effective partners in delivering the crispy texture that makes this a popular snack. It can go high or low depending on the occasion and is very easy to pull off. Tossed with mayonnaise, coated with seasoned panko, and roasted at high heat, the split pods become satisfyingly crunchy. Smoked paprika, lemon, and garlic stirred into mayonnaise yield a quick and flavorful dipping sauce and a fantastic offering for last-minute company.

- **1½ pounds fresh okra, halved lengthwise and larger pieces quartered**
- **5 tablespoons Blue Plate Mayonnaise**
- **¼ cup panko (Japanese breadcrumbs), lightly crushed**
- **1½ tablespoons all-purpose flour**
- **2 teaspoons no-salt-added Creole seasoning**
- **1½ teaspoons smoked paprika**
- **¾ teaspoon kosher salt**
- **½ teaspoon lemon zest**
- **¼ teaspoon garlic powder**
- **⅛ teaspoon cayenne pepper**
- **Smoky Mayonnaise (recipe follows)**
- **Lemon wedges, to serve**

1. Preheat oven to 450°F. Place 2 large rimmed baking sheets in oven while oven preheats.
2. In a large bowl, combine okra and mayonnaise, tossing to coat.
3. In a small bowl, whisk together panko, flour, Creole seasoning, paprika, salt, lemon zest, garlic powder, and cayenne. Sprinkle panko mixture evenly over okra mixture; toss to coat.
4. Place okra in a single layer on preheated baking sheets. Bake 16 to 20 minutes or until golden brown and crispy, stirring halfway through baking. Place on a serving platter. Serve immediately with Smoky Mayonnaise and lemon wedges.

Smoky Mayonnaise

Makes about ½ cup

- **½ cup Blue Plate Mayonnaise**
- **½ teaspoon lemon zest**
- **2 tablespoons fresh lemon juice**
- **1 tablespoon smoked paprika, plus more for garnish**
- **1 clove garlic, grated**

1. In a small bowl, whisk together all ingredients until well combined. Garnish with smoked paprika, if desired.

CHAPTER 6

Sit Down and Stay Awhile

For the days when there is time to truly enjoy the experience of a carefully curated meal, and occasions when the dishes shared at the table are most often reserved to mark a special moment, we've got you. In the Gulf South, these are the dishes that invite you to linger and appreciate the opportunity to savor them together.

Creole Eggs Benedict

Makes 4 servings

This take on eggs Benedict, a brunch favorite, relies on Creole flavors for a decidedly Louisiana-centric flair. In place of standard Canadian bacon, smoky, garlicky andouille brings a deeply seasoned accent to the runny yolks of the poached eggs. Cut butterfly-style for maximum searing surface, the andouille sausage develops a deeply browned, caramelized flavor. Hollandaise sauce is the signature of any version of eggs Benedict. As an emulsified egg-yolk base, Blue Plate Mayonnaise makes this Shortcut Hollandaise version simple, fast, and foolproof: There's no worry of the sauce breaking or overheating, no separating eggs yolks from their whites, and no cumbersome double boiler set up. You've got this handled with just a bowl and a whisk.

1 tablespoon white distilled vinegar
2 teaspoons salt
4 large eggs
1 (16-ounce) package andouille sausage
2 English muffins, sliced horizontally
Shortcut Hollandaise (page 220)
Garnish: chopped fresh chives, paprika

1. Fill a medium saucepan with water up to 2 inches from the top. Add vinegar and salt, and bring to a simmer. Stir the water in a clockwise motion, and crack the eggs, 1 at a time, into the pot, allowing the swirling water to envelop the eggs. Cook for 3 to 4 minutes or until the whites are opaque and the yolks are still runny. Using a slotted spoon, remove each egg from the water, and let drain on a paper towel–lined plate.
2. Heat a large skillet over medium heat. Cut the andouille sausage into 4-inch pieces, and then cut each piece in half lengthwise. Cut halves lengthwise three-fourths of the way through. Place andouille, cut sides down, in skillet, and cook until golden and crispy, 3 to 5 minutes. Turn, and cook until crispy, 3 to 5 minutes.
3. Toast the English muffins, and place halves on a platter. Top each half with a piece of andouille sausage and a poached egg. Spoon the Shortcut Hollandaise over the top. Serve immediately. Garnish with chives and paprika, if desired.

The Creamiest Scrambled Eggs and Crispy Potato Hash Browns

Makes 3 to 4 servings

For next-level scrambled eggs, the key is egg yolk–based mayonnaise. It doesn't take much—about 2 teaspoons mayonnaise per egg—to amp up the creamy texture. It's a formula worth remembering and is a far better move than whisking in milk or cream, which can dilute the rich egg taste that you're after. Whisking in the mayonnaise keeps the scramble loose while it cooks to ensure a fluffy texture and guard against a dry, overcooked result. Hash browns are best when their exterior is evenly golden and crisp while the inside steams to become melt-in-your-mouth tender. When cooking hash browns, butter used as the frying fat will quickly burn (save it for flavor boosting), and vegetable oil brings virtually no flavor, but mayonnaise gets you right where you want with tangy richness to boot. Best of all, this breakfast is special enough to serve to weekend company but is also easy enough to whip together on a busy Tuesday morning. Sensational is that simple.

6 large eggs
¼ cup Blue Plate Mayonnaise
Salt, to taste
2 tablespoons unsalted butter, cubed, divided
Garnish: snipped fresh chives

1. In a medium bowl, whisk together eggs, mayonnaise, and salt to taste until well combined and no white streaks are left.

2. In a large, heavy-bottomed skillet, melt 1 tablespoon butter over medium-low heat. Add egg mixture. Cook, stirring constantly with a rubber spatula, until eggs begin to set, about 2 minutes. Stir in remaining butter. Cook, stirring constantly, until fluffy and cooked but still soft, 1 to 2 more minutes. Spoon onto plates, and top with snipped chives, if desired.

Crispy Potato Hash Browns

Makes 3 to 4 servings

1 pound or 4 cups peeled coarsely grated russet potatoes
¾ teaspoon kosher salt
⅛ teaspoon ground black pepper
6 tablespoons Blue Plate Mayonnaise, divided
Garnish: flaky sea salt

1. Place potatoes in a medium colander. Rinse under cold water until water runs clear. Drain. Place potatoes in center of a clean kitchen towel. Fold over long sides of towel; twist ends tightly to squeeze out excess moisture. In a large bowl, toss together potatoes, kosher salt, and pepper.

2. Heat a 10-inch nonstick skillet over medium-low heat until hot, 1 to 2 minutes. Add 3 tablespoons mayonnaise to skillet, and spread the mayonnaise in the skillet using a small rubber spatula. Carefully add potato mixture to skillet, pressing with spatula. Cook, without stirring, until golden brown underneath, about 10 minutes. Carefully flip hash browns using a large plate or rimless baking sheet, adding remaining 3 tablespoons mayonnaise to pan, and cook until golden brown, about 10 minutes more.

3. Carefully transfer hash browns to plates. Serve immediately. Garnish with sea salt, if desired.

Pelicans are a beloved sight along the marshes, wetlands, and coastlines of the Gulf, drawn to waters rich with catfish, redfish, oysters, and shrimp. American White Pelicans (pictured) winter along the Gulf, having traveled south from breeding grounds much farther inland. They literally herd fish into shallow water before scooping them into their beaks to eat. You'll see brown pelicans, Louisiana's protected state bird, soaring year-round over the Gulf waters to spot and then dive for their catch. These waters and their abundance sustain these special coastal birds the same way they have fed and influenced the area's food culture for centuries.

Shrimp and Grits

Makes 4 servings

One of the most ubiquitous Southern dishes has to be shrimp and grits. It has a foothold in almost every Southern region, including the Gulf South, where coastal waters, from Texas to Florida, are teeming with shrimp. Butter and Creole seasoning cooked with the shrimp create the drippings and the base for the tomato and andouille pan sauce that tops the dish. Succulent seared shrimp crown it. The grits cook over low heat and need only water and salt to coax them to their creamiest potential. Gruyère and Cheddar cheeses bring sharp, nutty depth, and mayonnaise adds a richness and tang that butter alone can't deliver, leaving the grits silky and loose to the last bite.

Cheese Grits

4 cups water
¼ teaspoon salt
1 cup stone-ground yellow or white grits (not instant)
½ cup Blue Plate Mayonnaise
¾ cup freshly shredded Gruyère cheese
¾ cup freshly shredded sharp Cheddar cheese
Ground black pepper, to taste

Shrimp

2 tablespoons unsalted butter, divided
1 tablespoon olive oil
1 pound fresh large shrimp, peeled and deveined
¼ teaspoon Creole seasoning
½ cup finely diced andouille or other smoked sausage
½ cup finely diced sweet onion
¼ cup finely diced celery
¼ teaspoon dried thyme leaves
1 (15-ounce) can diced tomatoes, undrained
1 teaspoon fresh lemon juice

1. Make the grits: Bring 4 cups water and salt to a boil in a 3-quart saucepan. Stir in grits. Turn heat to low. Cook, stirring often, 20 minutes or for the time indicated on the package, until grits are tender. Stir in mayonnaise, cheeses, and a generous amount of pepper. Mix well. Cover to keep warm.

2. Make the shrimp: In a 12-inch skillet, melt 1 tablespoon butter and oil over medium-high heat. Season shrimp with Creole seasoning, and add to skillet. Cook until shrimp start to turn pink on one side, 1 to 2 minutes, then flip and cook just until opaque, 30 seconds to 1 minute. Do not overcook. Remove shrimp with a slotted spoon, and reserve in a bowl. Do not wipe skillet clean.

3. Reduce heat to medium. Add sausage, onion, celery, and thyme to drippings in skillet. Cook until onion is translucent, about 5 minutes.

4. Add remaining 1 tablespoon butter and tomatoes with juice; cook until mixture starts to reduce, about 5 minutes. Add lemon juice, shrimp, and any juices the shrimp have given off. Cook until shrimp are warmed through completely, about 5 minutes more. Serve shrimp and pan sauce immediately over the warm grits. Refrigerate leftovers for up to 2 days.

Note: The grits can be made up to one day ahead. Coat a 1½-quart baking dish with nonstick cooking spray, and transfer grits mixture to the dish. Cover with foil, and refrigerate up to 1 day. Remove from the refrigerator 1 hour before serving; do not remove foil. Preheat oven to 350°F. Bake grits, covered, until warmed through, 20 to 30 minutes. Uncover and stir well before serving.

CONTRIBUTOR

Jolie Meaux
Blogger and
Recipe Developer

Lafayette, LA

Jolie Meaux has always been known as a nurturer when it comes to feeding people, from her high school friends, her family, her community, to even Anthony Bourdain. A cook who learned from her grandmother and aunts, Meaux is also a self-taught recipe developer whose popular blog *Porch, Wine & Gravy* is resplendent with recipes rooted in the dishes and food traditions of Cajun Louisiana. Meaux has completed extensive research into the historic methods and ingredients behind Cajun cooking with the goal of keeping traditions alive and staying authentic. On most Sundays, you'll find her at her Lafayette home, hosting suppers to share with friends and family.

Chicken and Sausage Gumbo with Potato Salad

Makes 10 to 12 servings

Gumbo is the official state dish of Louisiana, and its flavor base draws from French, Spanish, African, Acadian, and Native American foodways, a convergence that makes it one of the most culturally layered dishes in the Gulf South. Jolie Meaux's version is a testament to those traditions and her Acadian roots. As such, she cooks her roux until it reaches a deep color that resembles dark chocolate. Don't rush the process, or you run the risk of burning rather than developing the nutty, slightly bitter flavor. Chicken thighs and sausage are seared, and then simmered in that deeply flavored base until tender, lending meaty intensity to the gumbo. Serving gumbo over rice or with potato salad—or both—is hotly debated in Louisiana. Purists insist on rice, while many in Acadiana believe only potato salad will do, and others do both. Meaux traditionally serves her gumbo with potato salad but will sometimes serve it with Potato Salad Croquettes for special occasions.

1½ pounds smoked sausage, sliced
1½ pounds boneless, skinless chicken thighs, cut into bite-size pieces
½ cup vegetable oil (or use rendered fat left over from meat in Step 2)
½ cup all-purpose flour
2 cups chopped onion
1 cup chopped celery
½ cup chopped green bell pepper
2 tablespoons minced garlic
6 cups warm chicken stock (store-bought or homemade)
2 teaspoons Cajun seasoning
Salt and ground black pepper, to taste
Cooked white rice, Southern Potato Salad or Potato Salad Croquettes (page 125), sliced green onion, to serve

1. In a large Dutch oven, cook sausage over medium heat until browned, about 4 minutes. Remove and set aside, leaving drippings in the pot.
2. Add chicken to the same pot, and cook until lightly browned, about 5 minutes (it does not need to be fully cooked through). Remove, and set aside.
3. If the rendered fat in the pot is less than ½ cup, add enough vegetable oil to reach ½ cup total fat. Or remove drippings, and use total amount of oil. Whisk in flour, and cook over medium heat, whisking constantly, until the roux reaches a deep chocolate brown color, 20 to 25 minutes. Adjust heat as needed to prevent burning.
4. Add onion, celery, and bell pepper. Cook, stirring frequently, until vegetables are softened, 8 to 10 minutes. Add garlic, and cook, stirring constantly, until fragrant, about 1 minute.
5. Gradually add warm stock, stirring constantly until smooth and fully incorporated. Bring to a simmer, and cook, stirring occasionally, until slightly thickened, about 45 minutes.
6. Return sausage and chicken to the pot. Add Cajun seasoning, and simmer until chicken is fully cooked and tender, 20 to 25 minutes. Skim any excess fat from the surface, if needed.
7. Season with salt and black pepper to taste. Serve over rice, with Southern Potato Salad or Potato Salad Croquettes, or both. Sprinkle with green onion.

Roux, made by slowly cooking flour and fat together, is the foundation of countless sauces and stews. The stage it's taken to depends on the dish being prepared. Some dishes rely on a pale golden roux, like pot pies and gratins, while others, like gumbo and étouffée, feature a darker roux with caramel and chocolate tones that lend deep, savory, nutty flavor. Method matters here: Slow development and continual stirring prevent scorching, which will bring in bitterness.

Beef Daube Pot Pies

Makes 6 servings

Daube, a braised beef recipe, came to New Orleans with French Creole settlers and is cherished for its rich and savory flavors. Reimagined as individual pot pies, the dish takes on a comforting bistro character with tender beef and a silky red wine sauce sealed beneath a flaky puff pastry crust. As a marinade, mayonnaise tenderizes and seasons the eye round, which becomes tender after braising in red wine with porcini mushrooms and thyme. The meat and resulting sauce are portioned into individual crocks, topped with puff pastry, and baked. Thanks to a brush of egg yolk–based mayonnaise in place of a standard egg wash, the flaky crust gets a richer, deeper golden finish than a whole egg alone would deliver.

1½ cups boiling water
½ cup dried porcini mushrooms
3½ pounds boneless well-marbled eye round, cut into 1-inch cubes
⅓ cup Blue Plate Mayonnaise, plus more for brushing
4½ teaspoons kosher salt, divided
1½ teaspoons ground black pepper, divided
¼ cup vegetables oil, divided
2 cups chopped celery root
2 cups chopped onion
1½ cups chopped celery
3 cloves garlic, minced
1½ cups beef stock
1½ cups dry red wine, such as cabernet sauvignon
3 tablespoons tomato paste
3 tablespoons brandy
1 tablespoon minced fresh thyme
1 tablespoon minced fresh rosemary
4 bay leaves
2 cups chopped carrots
3 tablespoons chopped fresh parsley
1 tablespoon red wine vinegar
1½ sheets frozen puff pastry, thawed
Garnish: fresh thyme sprigs

1. In a medium bowl, combine 1½ cups boiling water and mushrooms. Let stand until softened, about 30 minutes. Strain through a fine-mesh sieve, reserving liquid. Chop mushrooms, and set aside.
2. In medium bowl, toss together beef cubes, ⅓ cup mayonnaise, 2 teaspoons salt, and 1 teaspoon pepper. Let marinate in refrigerator for 1 hour or up to overnight.
3. Preheat oven to 350°F.
4. In a large Dutch oven, heat 2 tablespoons oil over medium-high heat. Add one-third of beef mixture to pan; cook until browned, about 5 minutes. Remove from pan with a slotted spoon. Repeat with remaining beef mixture.
5. Add remaining 2 tablespoons oil to pan. Add celery root, onion, and chopped celery; cook until lightly browned, about 8 minutes. Add garlic; cook 1 minute. Add chopped mushrooms, mushroom liquid, beef, beef stock, wine, tomato paste, brandy, thyme, rosemary, and bay leaves to Dutch oven; stir well. Cover, and bake until beef is tender, about 1 hour 30 minutes; add carrot, and cook until beef is very tender, 30 minutes more. Discard bay leaves. Stir in parsley, vinegar, 2 teaspoons salt, and remaining ½ teaspoon pepper. Remove from oven.
6. Increase oven temperature to 425°F.
7. Place 6 (1½-cup) ovenproof soup bowls on a large rimmed baking sheet. Spoon stew into bowls, leaving ½-inch space at the top. On a lightly floured surface, unfold puff pastry; cut into 6 squares. Brush edges of bowls with mayonnaise. Place pastry over hot stew. Cut an "X" in the top of pastry. Brush pastry with mayonnaise. Sprinkle with remaining ½ teaspoon salt. Bake until pastry is puffed and golden brown, about 10 minutes. Garnish with thyme sprigs, if desired.

CONTRIBUTOR

Michael Gulotta
Chef Partner
Tana

New Orleans, LA

Michael Gulotta grew up in New Orleans and worked in the Italian Riviera and Germany's Black Forest before returning home. As chef de cuisine at Restaurant August, one of the most celebrated fine-dining restaurants in New Orleans, he helped rebuild and reopen the kitchen after Hurricane Katrina with a commitment to building strong and supportive relationships with local farmers and purveyors. At Tana, his food blends the flavors of his New Orleans Sicilian roots and his experience working in Liguria, Italy. A five-time James Beard semifinalist and *Food & Wine* Best New Chef, Gulotta is one of the most compelling voices in New Orleans cooking today.

Braciolone

Makes 6 to 8 servings

Braciolone is a showstopper. A large, dramatic stuffed beef roll that simmers in a robust red gravy, it's a special-occasion dish, so don't skimp on choosing quality ingredients. The stuffing includes a sublime mix of roasted garlic, Parmesan, breadcrumbs, and hard-cooked eggs, bound together with mayonnaise that helps to ensure the roll slices cleanly at serving. Chef Michael Gulotta calls for chuck flap, a well-marbled cut that sits near the ribeye and shares some of its richness, making it a natural choice for a long braise. Butterflied and pounded thin, the meat is filled, rolled tightly, and tied so that every slice reveals a beautiful spiral of filling. If you can't find the flap at your butcher shop, ask for a cut of Denver steak.

Filling

- 3 large eggs, hard-cooked (see page 92) and chopped
- ½ cup Italian breadcrumbs
- ¼ cup finely grated Parmesan cheese, plus more for garnish
- ¼ cup Blue Plate Mayonnaise
- 2 tablespoons finely chopped fresh flat-leaf parsley, plus more for garnish
- 4 cloves roasted garlic, minced
- ¾ teaspoon kosher salt
- ⅛ teaspoon crushed red pepper

Meat

- 1 (2-pound) chuck flap
- 1 teaspoon kosher salt
- ½ teaspoon ground black pepper
- 2 tablespoons Blue Plate Mayonnaise
- Red Gravy (page 181)
- Angel hair pasta, to serve

1. Make the filling: In a medium bowl, combine eggs, breadcrumbs, cheese, mayonnaise, parsley, garlic, salt, and red pepper; mix until well combined and spreadable. Set aside.

2. Make the meat: Place beef on a cutting board. Using a sharp knife, slice horizontally through the center, keeping the knife parallel to the board and leaving about a ½-inch hinge. Open flat like a book, cover with plastic wrap, and pound to an even ¼-inch thickness. Season with salt and pepper.

3. Spread the filling evenly over the beef, leaving a 1-inch border on one long side. Roll the meat tightly, starting from the long side closest to you, keeping the filling enclosed. Tie with butcher's twine at 2-inch intervals. Coat the outside lightly and evenly with mayonnaise.

4. Heat a large braising pan over medium-high heat. Sear braciolone on all sides until golden brown, about 2 minutes per side.

5. Add Red Gravy to pan, bring to a simmer, reduce heat to low, and cover tightly. Cook for 1 hour to 1 hour 30 minutes, or until tender and an instant-read thermometer registers at least 145°F, turning occasionally.

6. Remove from pan; let rest 10 to 15 minutes. Slice into 1-inch pieces; serve with pasta and Red Gravy. Garnish with Parmesan and parsley, if desired.

IN THE LATE 1800S, Sicilian families began immigrating to New Orleans, bringing their food, cooking styles, and cultural influence to the region, and those influences are still a strong part of the city. By the turn of the century, groceries, produce markets, pasta factories, and bakeries had become a vital part of the French Quarter. One particular part, nicknamed "Little Palermo" after the capital of Sicily, became known for its ingredients and iconic foods like muffulettas and red gravy. Over the years, families spread out to the Mississippi Delta and the broader Gulf South, extending Italian influence.

Red Gravy

Makes about 4 cups

- 2 tablespoons extra-virgin olive oil
- 1 red bell pepper, diced
- 4 cloves garlic, minced
- 2 teaspoons granulated sugar
- 2 (28-ounce) cans peeled whole tomatoes, coarsely crushed
- 1 orange, halved
- 2 tablespoons chopped fresh basil
- ⅛ teaspoon crushed red pepper
- ⅛ teaspoon ground black pepper

1. In a large pot, heat olive oil over medium heat. Add bell pepper and garlic; cook until softened, stirring often, about 5 to 7 minutes. Add sugar, and cook 1 to 2 minutes until well combined and slightly darkened.

2. Add tomatoes, orange halves, basil, red pepper, and black pepper; simmer, uncovered, stirring occasionally, over medium heat until slightly thickened, 30 to 45 minutes. Remove and discard orange halves.

Sicilian immigrants brought the tradition of building altars honoring St. Joseph when they arrived in Louisiana in the 1800s. The Catholic custom spread across the Gulf South to communities in Texas, Mississippi, and beyond. Altars piled high with food offerings, including fava beans, breads shaped like carpenter's tools, whole fish, and fruit, with a statue of St. Joseph at the top, are built each year on March 19. Visitors arrive at churches to pray, light candles, and leave written petitions offering thanks and seeking good health, safety, and relief from hardships.

St. Joseph, Pray for us
Gail Savoie

Fried Chicken and Braised Collards with Smoked Ham Hocks

Makes 8 to 10 servings

A brine of buttermilk and mayonnaise enhances this platter of juicy, deeply seasoned fried chicken. The acidity in the mixture tenderizes the meat and locks in moisture during frying. Dredged in seasoned flour and fried, each piece emerges from the pan with an irresistible craggy, crunchy, golden-brown crust. Serve the rich chicken with collard greens that simmer long enough to create a potlikker for a bright, savory contrast. Just like hot sauce, mayonnaise can be served as a condiment at the table to stir into the collards. It's a preference that people in some regions of the South and Appalachia like for the added creaminess it brings and a tang that echoes vinegar.

3½ cups whole buttermilk, divided
2 cups Blue Plate Mayonnaise
⅓ cup kosher salt, plus more for seasoning
2 tablespoons granulated sugar
1 tablespoon Louisiana-style hot sauce
1½ teaspoons ground black pepper
5 pounds bone-in, skin-on chicken pieces
Vegetable oil, for frying
3 cups all-purpose flour
1 tablespoon Cajun seasoning
Braised Collards with Smoked Ham Hocks (recipe follows)

1. In a large bowl, combine 2 cups buttermilk, mayonnaise, salt, sugar, hot sauce, and black pepper. Add chicken; cover, and refrigerate 4 hours or up to overnight. Drain chicken, discarding liquid. Pat chicken dry with paper towels.

2. In a large, deep-sided cast-iron skillet or Dutch oven, pour oil to a depth of 2 inches, and heat over medium heat until a deep-fry thermometer registers 350°F.

3. In a shallow dish, whisk together flour and Cajun seasoning. In another shallow dish, add remaining 1½ cups buttermilk. Dredge chicken in flour mixture, shaking off excess. Dip in buttermilk, letting excess drip off. Dredge chicken in flour mixture again, shaking off excess.

4. Working in batches, fry chicken, turning occasionally, until a meat thermometer inserted in thickest sections registers 165°F, 15 to 20 minutes. Let drain on a wire rack set over paper towels. Sprinkle with salt, if desired. Serve with Braised Collards with Smoked Ham Hocks.

Braised Collards with Smoked Ham Hocks

Makes 4 cups

2 tablespoons vegetable oil
2 smoked ham hocks
2 cups chopped yellow onion
3 tablespoons minced garlic
1 pound chopped fresh collard greens, stemmed
6 cups chicken broth
2 tablespoons cane vinegar
Salt and ground black pepper, to taste
Louisiana-style hot sauce, to serve
Blue Plate Mayonnaise, to serve

1. In a large Dutch oven, heat oil over medium heat. Score ham hocks, and add to pot. Cook, turning occasionally, until browned on all sides, 6 to 8 minutes. Remove from pot.

2. Add onion and garlic to pot; cook over medium heat until softened and aromatic, about 4 minutes. Gradually add greens and broth, letting each batch of greens wilt down before adding more. Return ham hocks to pot; bring to a boil. Reduce heat, cover, and simmer until greens and ham hocks are tender, about 1 hour 30 minutes.

3. Remove ham hocks; let cool enough to handle. Remove meat from ham hocks, discarding skin and bones. Return ham to collards. Stir in vinegar. Season with salt and pepper to taste. Cook, uncovered, for 15 minutes. Serve warm with hot sauce and a dollop of mayonnaise, if desired.

CONTRIBUTOR

Roscoe Hall
Chef and Artist

Birmingham, AL

Roscoe Hall is a Birmingham-based chef and artist who got his first glimpse of the culinary world from his grandfather's legendary Dreamland Bar-B-Que in Tuscaloosa, Alabama. He splits his time between painting and cooking and has worked at prestigious restaurants including Chez Panisse and Momofuku Ssäm Bar. In Birmingham, he is regarded as one of the city's most creative forces, installing his artwork at restaurants and galleries. An ambassador for Sweet Grown Alabama, an agricultural advocacy organization, Hall is committed to supporting local farmers and producers. He has ground crops like turmeric and collard greens into handmade pigments to tell the story of the region on canvas.

Satsuma Roasted Game Hens

Makes 4 hens

Lacquered and golden, these roasted whole game hens are centerpiece worthy when placed on a platter and paired with satsuma oranges and fresh herbs. Roscoe Hall employs mayonnaise to do three jobs in this recipe: act as a seasoning, a basting glaze, and the base for a white sauce designed to highlight the citrus. The marinade incorporates fragrant satsuma zest and tangerine juice along with smoked paprika and cane syrup that seasons the birds with a smoky, sweet essence. The glaze, made thick enough by the mayonnaise so it adheres well to the hens, is brushed on periodically as they roast. So vibrant it will become a go-to for everyday chicken, the white sauce might just become a standout on its own. You can use Sumo Citrus, clementines, or mandarins if you can't find satsumas.

- 4 game hens
- 1 tablespoon kosher salt
- 1½ cups Blue Plate Mayonnaise
- 2 teaspoons satsuma zest
- 3 tablespoons fresh satsuma juice
- 1 tablespoon cane syrup or firmly packed brown sugar
- 1 tablespoon smoked paprika
- 2 teaspoons ground black pepper
- 2 teaspoons soy sauce
- 1 teaspoon onion powder
- 2 cloves garlic, grated
- 1 to 2 tablespoons cane vinegar
- Satsuma White Barbecue Sauce (recipe follows), to serve

1. Preheat oven to 400°F.
2. Place hens on wire racks over 2 foil-lined rimmed baking sheets. Lightly salt hens on all sides.
3. In a medium bowl, whisk together 1½ cups mayonnaise, satsuma zest, satsuma juice, cane syrup, paprika, pepper, soy sauce, onion powder, and garlic. Remove ½ cup mayonnaise mixture, and set aside. Coat hens evenly with remaining mayonnaise mixture.
4. Roast hens until skin is lightly browned, 25 minutes.
5. In a small bowl, whisk together reserved ½ cup mayonnaise mixture and cane vinegar to create a lacquer; brush lightly over hens. Roast hens until an instant-read thermometer registers 165°F, 10 to 15 minutes. Brush once more with the mayonnaise-vinegar mixture.
6. Alternatively, for darker, crispier skin, increase the oven temperature to broil, and broil until lightly browned, about 3 minutes. Let hens rest 5 to 10 minutes before serving. Serve with Satsuma White Barbecue Sauce.

Satsuma White Barbecue Sauce

Makes 1½ cups

- 1 cup Blue Plate Mayonnaise
- ¼ cup fresh satsuma juice
- 2 tablespoons cane vinegar
- 1 tablespoon ground black pepper
- ½ to 1 teaspoon kosher salt
- ½ teaspoon onion powder
- 2 tablespoons water

1. In a medium bowl, whisk together mayonnaise, satsuma juice, cane vinegar, pepper, salt, and onion powder until smooth. Thin with water, 1 tablespoon at a time, until it reaches a pourable consistency. Spoon sauce over hens or serve on the side.

Satsumas are a variety of mandarin orange that arrived in the Gulf South from Japan in the late nineteenth to the early twentieth centuries. Named for the former Japanese province with the same name, they flourished in the southernmost Louisiana parishes where the climate closely resembles their Japanese origin. Ripe from late September through early December—an eagerly anticipated season—the citrus is treasured for its sweetness, low acid, and easy-to-peel skin. The Louisiana satsuma is a designated Slow Food Ark of Taste ingredient, a listing that brings both recognition and a call to action to preserve the fruit by raising awareness, supporting small producers, and encouraging chefs and consumers to use them.

From rivers and bayous to tidal creeks and sloughs, the Gulf South's interconnected waterways create a stunningly beautiful landscape. Whether through hunting, fishing, or simply enjoying time on the water, people are invited to slow down and appreciate the gifts offered and the peaceful surroundings.

Roast Duck with Orange-Cane Syrup Sauce

Makes 4 to 6 servings

Duck has long been a prized protein on Gulf South tables, hunted in rich wetlands, marshes, and areas across the South. Preparation is key to success: After a day of air-drying the duck in the refrigerator, you'll blanch it in boiling water to render the fat. The effort is a critical step for getting the skin crisp. The bird roasts simply seasoned with paprika and mayonnaise spread inside the cavity so that it self-bastes and flavors the dark meat. The sauce, built around the flavors of cane syrup and orange juice, is whisked with mayonnaise creating a silky, stable emulsion. For a complete dinner, serve this rich duck with roasted vegetables and a simple chicory salad.

- **1 (4- to 5-pound) duck**
- **1 tablespoon plus ½ teaspoon kosher salt, divided**
- **½ teaspoon ground black pepper**
- **1 tablespoon vegetable oil**
- **¼ cup minced shallots**
- **1 large orange, zested and juiced**
- **3 tablespoons Steen's cane syrup**
- **1 tablespoon orange blossom honey**
- **5 tablespoons Blue Plate Mayonnaise, divided**
- **1 tablespoon chopped fresh sage**
- **1 tablespoon chopped fresh tarragon**
- **2 teaspoons white vinegar**
- **⅛ to ¼ teaspoon cayenne pepper**
- **½ teaspoon plus ⅛ teaspoon paprika, divided**
- **6 quarts water**
- **3 tablespoons vegetable oil**
- **2 sprigs fresh tarragon**
- **2 sprigs fresh sage**

Garnish: orange slices, fresh sage leaves, fresh tarragon leaves

1. Rinse duck, and pat dry with paper towels. Place duck, breast side up, on a roasting rack in a roasting pan. Using the tip of a paring knife or a fork, pierce duck skin all over (front and back), making sure you slide the knife tip under the skin and not into the meat. (Do not pierce duck breast holding the knife perpendicular or meat may dry out quickly when cooking.) In a small bowl, whisk together 1 tablespoon salt and black pepper. Rub salt mixture all over the outside and inside of duck. Place in refrigerator, uncovered, for at least 24 hours or up to 48 hours.

2. In a medium saucepan, heat oil over medium heat until hot, 1 to 2 minutes. Add shallots, and cook, stirring frequently, until translucent. Add ½ cup orange juice, cane syrup, honey, and remaining ½ teaspoon salt; increase heat to medium-high, and allow mixture to come to a boil. Reduce heat, and simmer until thickened, about 20 minutes. Whisk in 3 tablespoons mayonnaise, 1 tablespoon at a time, until well combined. Whisk in 1 teaspoon orange zest, sage, tarragon, vinegar, cayenne, and ⅛ teaspoon paprika. Remove sauce from heat, and allow to cool completely.

3. Preheat oven to 425°F.

4. In a large stockpot set over high heat, bring 6 quarts water to a rolling boil. Carefully submerge duck in boiling water, and cook for 5 minutes. (This renders off excess duck fat and firms up the skin.)

5. Using long tongs, carefully remove duck from water, and return to prepared rack. Allow to cool for 10 minutes, and pat outside and inside of duck dry with paper towels.

6. In a small bowl, whisk together oil and remaining ½ teaspoon paprika. Rub half of oil mixture all over outside and inside of duck. Rub inside of duck with remaining 2 tablespoons mayonnaise, and stuff with tarragon and sage sprigs.

7. Place duck, breast side down, on prepared rack, and roast for 20 minutes. Carefully turn duck, breast side up, and roast until lightly golden brown, 25 minutes more.

8. Reduce oven temperature to 350°F. Using a silicone spatula, brush duck skin with remaining half of oil mixture. Continue roasting until an instant-read thermometer registers 170°F (for medium) to 180°F (for well done) at the leg and thigh joint, 45 to 50 minutes.

9. Remove from oven, and let rest at room temperature for 15 minutes. Rewarm sauce in saucepan, and serve with duck. Garnish with orange slices, sage, and tarragon, if desired.

Rabbit and Dumplings

Makes 6 servings

Built around tender rabbit and a vegetable stew of leeks, carrots, celery, and onion enriched with heavy cream and white wine, this easy one-pot meal's co-stars are the fluffy dumplings. They're delicious thanks to mayonnaise taking the place of butter or shortening, making them rich but light. Dropped into the pot to simmer along with the rabbit until they puff and float, it's just the right bite against the creamy base. Mayonnaise also serves an additional purpose: Heated as the cooking fat for the leeks, onion, and celery, it lends its own character to the base as the stew is built.

1 (3.2- to 4-pound) cleaned rabbit
1 yellow onion, quartered
1 cup celery pieces
4¼ teaspoons kosher salt, divided
2½ teaspoons ground black pepper, divided
8 cups water
¼ cup plus 3 tablespoons Blue Plate Mayonnaise, divided
2 cups sliced leeks
½ cup chopped yellow onion
½ cup chopped celery
2 teaspoons chopped garlic
¼ cup all-purpose flour
½ cup dry white wine
1 cup heavy whipping cream, room temperature
2 cups half-moon sliced carrots
1 tablespoon finely chopped fresh rosemary
¼ cup chopped fresh parsley
1½ cups self-rising flour
⅔ cup whole milk
¼ teaspoon garlic powder

1. In a large Dutch oven, add rabbit, onion, celery pieces, 2 teaspoons salt, and 2 teaspoons pepper. Cover with 8 cups water. Cover and cook over medium heat until an instant-read thermometer inserted in thickest portion of rabbit registers 200°F, at least 2 hours. Let cool in broth. Remove rabbit, and shred meat. (This should yield at least 3 cups shredded rabbit.) Reserve 6 cups broth.

2. Heat a large Dutch oven over medium heat. Add 3 tablespoons mayonnaise, and cook until melted. Add leeks, onion, and celery; cook, stirring often, until vegetables are tender, 5 to 10 minutes. Stir in garlic, and cook 1 minute. Stir in all-purpose flour, and cook 1 minute. Stir in wine, and cook until thickened. Whisk in reserved broth and cream. Stir in carrots and rosemary; cook until thickened and carrots are tender. Stir in rabbit, parsley, 1½ teaspoons salt, and remaining ½ teaspoon pepper. Reduce heat to a simmer.

3. In a medium bowl, whisk together self-rising flour, milk, remaining ¼ cup mayonnaise, remaining ¾ teaspoon salt, and garlic powder until well combined. Using a 1 tablespoon spring-loaded scoop, drop dumplings, a few at a time, in simmering stew. (Do not stir.) Cover and gently shake pot in a circular motion; cook until dumplings float, 3 to 4 minutes. Serve immediately.

Every pot has a purpose. From cast-iron skillets that go from stovetop to oven and even straight to the table, to sturdy Dutch ovens and vintage Magnalite roasters built for long, slow cooking, each piece is chosen for the job it does best. Quality cookware serves families for generations.

Root Beer-Glazed Ham

Makes 10 to 12 servings

Barq's root beer, a Biloxi, Mississippi, original founded in 1898 and later headquartered in New Orleans, has long been a popular ingredient paired with ham in the Gulf South. The root beer, whisked together with mayonnaise, Creole mustard, and hot sauce, creates a glaze that sticks to the scored ham's surface and caramelizes for a mahogany finish. Cloves complement the sweet, spiced glaze and release their aromatic oils as the ham bakes. Baste often to develop a gorgeous, glistening gloss. While you might be tempted to steal a little taste straight out of the oven, take care—it will be molten hot, and can burn your fingers and tongue. Give the ham 15 to 20 minutes for the root beer glaze to settle and cool.

1 (9-pound) fully cooked smoked ham shank
Whole cloves
1⅓ cups Barq's Root Beer, divided
⅔ cup Blue Plate Mayonnaise
1 tablespoon Creole mustard
1 teaspoon Louisiana-style hot sauce
Garnish: fresh rosemary sprigs

1. Preheat the oven to 300°F. Spray a roasting pan with cooking spray. Place ham in roasting pan.

2. Score the skin and fat of the ham by making long vertical and horizontal cuts. Place a whole clove in the center of each scored square. Pour 1 cup root beer over ham. Bake for 1 hour.

3. Increase oven temperature to 325°F.

4. In a medium bowl, whisk together mayonnaise, remaining ⅓ cup root beer, mustard, and hot sauce. Baste ham with the mayonnaise mixture.

5. Continue baking and basting ham occasionally, about every 20 minutes, with the mayonnaise mixture until ham is thoroughly heated, about 1 hour 20 minutes more. Loosely cover the ham with foil as needed to prevent overbrowning. Garnish with rosemary sprigs, if desired.

Creole Cornbread Stuffing

Makes 9 to 12 servings

Andouille sausage, the Holy Trinity—onion, celery, and bell pepper—and fresh mustard greens give classic cornbread stuffing a bold and peppery flavor profile that just might become a new holiday regular on your table. It works as well alongside a glazed ham or a roast chicken as it does a turkey. Mayonnaise is the stabilizer in the custard, keeping the mixture of eggs, heavy cream, and milk cohesive as it bakes. You can make this stuffing a day in advance, preparing it through Step 5, and refrigerating it, covered, until ready to bake. You'll need to add the cream mixture about 20 minutes before baking, and let it sit at room temperature to soften the cornbread and to take the chill off.

Skillet Cornbread (page 233), cooled and cut into 1-inch cubes
1 tablespoon unsalted butter
1 tablespoon olive oil
½ pound andouille sausage, coarsely chopped
1 small yellow onion, chopped (about 1 cup)
1 stalk celery, chopped
½ red bell pepper, chopped
4 cups coarsely chopped fresh mustard greens
2 teaspoons Creole seasoning
2 cloves garlic, chopped
1 cup heavy whipping cream
1 cup whole milk
½ cup Blue Plate Mayonnaise
4 large eggs

1. Preheat oven to 350°F.
2. On a large rimmed baking sheet, arrange cornbread cubes in a single layer. Bake until lightly toasted, about 20 minutes, stirring once. Let cool.
3. Grease a 13x9-inch baking dish with 1 tablespoon butter. Set aside.
4. Heat olive oil in a large skillet over medium heat until hot. Add the andouille, and cook until browned and slightly rendered, 3 to 5 minutes. Add the onion, celery, and red bell pepper, and cook until softened, 2 to 3 minutes more. Add the mustard greens, Creole seasoning, and garlic, and cook, stirring frequently, 2 to 3 minutes more. Remove pan from heat, and set aside to cool.
5. Spread half of the cornbread cubes in the bottom of the prepared baking dish; top with sausage mixture and remaining half of the cornbread cubes.
6. Whisk together heavy cream, milk, mayonnaise, and eggs, mixing well. Pour the cream mixture over the cornbread in the dish. Let stand at least 20 minutes before baking so that the cream mixture softens the cornbread.
7. Cover with greased foil, and bake until heated through, 40 to 50 minutes. Remove foil halfway through cooking to let top brown. Allow to cool slightly, and serve warm.

Spring Vegetable Salad

Makes 6 servings

Every table benefits from a fresh salad. Here, asparagus, sugar snap peas, and rainbow carrots are blanched to lock in their vibrant colors and retain their snap. Blanch in batches to preserve each vegetable's distinct texture. Mayo-based Creamy Deviled Egg Vinaigrette or Creole Caesar Dressing will bring a rich contrast to the bright, fresh vegetables. Serve with one or both. Easily adapt this recipe to other seasons: Try cherry tomatoes, yellow squash, and cucumber in summer months; shaved fennel, Broccolini, and green beans in fall; and radicchio, endive, and cauliflower in winter.

- **10 cups water**
- **2 tablespoons salt**
- **1 bunch fresh asparagus, trimmed**
- **1 pound rainbow carrots**
- **1 (6-ounce) package fresh sugar snap peas, halved lengthwise**
- **½ head fresh red leaf lettuce, washed and trimmed**
- **6 assorted red and watermelon radishes, thinly sliced**
- **½ teaspoon kosher salt**
- **¼ teaspoon ground black pepper**
- **Creamy Deviled Egg Vinaigrette (page 216)**
- **Creole Caesar Dressing (page 217)**

1. In a large bowl, prepare an ice-water bath, and set aside.

2. In a medium saucepan, combine 10 cups water and salt; bring to a boil over high heat. Add asparagus, and cook until bright green, 2 to 3 minutes. Using kitchen tongs or a slotted spoon, remove asparagus from boiling water, and place in ice-water bath; drain, and set aside. Repeat process with carrots and snap peas.

3. On a large platter, arrange asparagus, carrots, snap peas, lettuce leaves, and radishes; sprinkle with salt and pepper. Serve immediately with Creamy Deviled Egg Vinaigrette, Creole Caesar Dressing, or both.

CHAPTER 7

The Secret's in the Sauce

Sauces, dressings, and dips may look like an "extra" or an afterthought, but they are the connective tissue that unifies a dish. Drizzled, tossed, or dipped, the magic is in the pairing. Whether you prefer them on the side or fully incorporated, here you'll find plenty of ways to uplift and augment your dishes. Consider these sauces as the paint, and the food you serve with them, the canvas.

The word remoulade gets tossed around a lot in New Orleans and around the Gulf. But what exactly is it? The herb-forward, tangy sauce originated in France and arrived on the shores of Louisiana with 18th-century French settlers. Created from a mayonnaise base (scratch-made back then), French remoulade is a cold sauce that includes mustard, capers, cornichons, shallots, and tarragon for a punchy flavor profile. Adopted and adapted by New Orleanians, local remoulade flavor shifted with the addition of Creole mustard, horseradish, cayenne, paprika, green onion, and celery and the omission of cornichons and shallots. Styles diverged into two main schools: white and red. In New Orleans, some people would argue that remoulade is made with ketchup, but this is a mayonnaise cookbook. In the Gulf South, remoulade is usually served as an accompaniment to seafood or fried foods. Following are three recipes that embody the New Orleans and Gulf Coast remoulade story.

New Orleans Remoulade

Makes about 1⅔ cups

Lemon and Creole mustard give this New Orleans-style sauce a vibrant brightness that's a natural matchup to the Crab Cakes on page 39. With pale pink undertones from paprika and cayenne, this distinctive sauce is one of Louisiana's defining remoulade styles. Serve this mayonnaise-based sauce in all the expected ways, whether with boiled or poached shrimp or fried foods or as a dip for crudités, but also consider it for a riff on a dressed po-boy, substituting it for plain mayo.

1. In a medium bowl, whisk together 1 cup Blue Plate Mayonnaise, 3 tablespoons minced celery, 3 tablespoons Creole mustard, 2 tablespoons minced green onion, 2 tablespoons prepared horseradish, 2 tablespoons fresh lemon juice, 1 tablespoon Worcestershire sauce, 2 teaspoons granulated sugar, 1 teaspoon paprika, ½ teaspoon kosher salt, and ¼ teaspoon cayenne pepper. Cover and refrigerate for 1 hour before using or for up to 1 week.

Classic Louisiana Remoulade

Makes about 1 cup

With finely chopped fresh tarragon, chives, and parsley, this bright, punchy remoulade is closest to the French original it's derived from. Capers add brininess, and fresh lemon zest and juice lend acidity and fragrance. You'll find the sauce featured in the Shrimp Remoulade on page 153. But don't stop there: Enjoy it alongside raw oysters, or toss it with matchsticks of raw celery root for céleri rémoulade, *the classic French bistro salad where the sauce first appeared.*

1. In a small bowl, whisk together ½ cup Blue Plate Mayonnaise, ¼ cup Dijon mustard, 3 tablespoons chopped capers, 2 tablespoons chopped fresh parsley, 1 tablespoon prepared horseradish, 1 tablespoon chopped fresh chives, 1 tablespoon chopped fresh tarragon, ½ teaspoon lightly packed lemon zest, 2 teaspoons fresh lemon juice, ¼ teaspoon kosher salt, and ¼ teaspoon cayenne pepper. Cover and refrigerate for 1 hour before using or for up to 3 days.

Lemon Remoulade

Makes about ¾ cup
Recipe by Lucas McKinney

1. In a small bowl, whisk together ½ cup Blue Plate Mayonnaise, 2 tablespoons finely chopped green onion, 2 teaspoons lemon zest, 2 tablespoons fresh lemon juice, 2 tablespoons Creole mustard, 1 tablespoon prepared horseradish, ¾ teaspoon Creole seasoning, ¼ teaspoon minced garlic, a pinch of dried thyme, and a pinch of cayenne pepper until smooth and well combined. Taste and adjust seasoning as needed. Chill at least 15 minutes before serving to let the flavors come together. Store in an airtight container in refrigerator for up to 5 days.

CONTRIBUTOR

Julie Vaucresson
Vaucresson's
Sausage Co.

New Orleans, LA

Remoulade in New Orleans is as much about the ingredients as it is the combining of cultures and histories, a concept that embodies the Vaucresson family. Julie and Vance Vaucresson run their cafe and deli, a Creole soul restaurant, serving the signature hot sausage the family has made for over 125 years alongside classic New Orleans dishes and their own homemade Creole mustard. The couple hail from two long-established New Orleans Creole families and embrace preserving the food culture and history of the Seventh Ward. Julie makes all the sauces served at the cafe, and her remoulade is a standout. Made with their house-made mustard, it brings zesty flavor to a wide range of dishes, including crab cakes, boudin balls, and shrimp remoulade.

Julie Vaucresson's Remoulade

Makes about 1½ cups

This Creole family recipe is rooted in more than a century of kitchen wisdom and delivers bold, smoky, and spicy flavors from Vaucresson's own Creole mustard, smoked paprika, and horseradish. Use it as a dipping sauce for hush puppies or crawfish, or serve it alongside your favorite fried seafood. And it is always great with the classics—boiled shrimp and crab cakes.

- 1 cup Blue Plate Mayonnaise
- ¼ cup Creole mustard
- 2 tablespoons prepared horseradish
- 2 teaspoons smoked paprika
- ½ teaspoon cayenne pepper
- ½ teaspoon ground black pepper
- ½ teaspoon granulated garlic
- ½ teaspoon granulated onion
- 1 tablespoon dill pickle juice
- ½ teaspoon fresh lemon juice
- ½ teaspoon minced garlic

1. In a medium bowl, whisk together mayonnaise, Creole mustard, horseradish, paprika, cayenne, black pepper, granulated garlic, and granulated onion, stirring until smooth and fully incorporated.
2. Stir in dill pickle juice, lemon juice, and minced garlic. Taste and adjust seasoning as needed.
3. Cover and refrigerate for at least 1 hour to let the flavors meld. Store in an airtight container in refrigerator for up to 5 days.

Garlic Aioli

Makes about ½ cup

This ancient sauce is classically made by blending fresh garlic and olive oil together until the two very different ingredients, a liquid and solid, emulsify. Mayonnaise, already an emulsification, speeds that process along here to become a thick, creamy sauce with a pungent, savory depth from both the garlic and a touch of Creole mustard. Aioli is delicious over blanched, steamed, or roasted vegetables, as a sandwich spread, or as a finishing sauce for grilled meats and all manner of seafood.

1. In a medium bowl, smash 5 cloves garlic to a paste. Add ½ cup Blue Plate Mayonnaise, 2 teaspoons fresh lemon juice, 1 teaspoon Creole mustard, ⅛ teaspoon kosher salt, and ⅛ teaspoon ground black pepper, stirring with a whisk until well combined. Refrigerate until ready to use.

Herb Aioli

Prepare the Garlic Aioli as directed, substituting ¼ teaspoon Dijon mustard for the Creole mustard and stirring in ¼ cup chopped fresh parsley and 2 tablespoons chopped fresh chives. Makes about ½ cup. Refrigerate until ready to use. Be sure to look for Peter Nguyen's spicy take on aioli incorporating chili crisp on page 79.

Mayo-Mustard Sauce

Makes about 1½ cups

The bold, tangy notes of Creole mustard and a peppery hit of hot sauce take a front seat in this simple-to-make condiment. Serve it with baked ham or on a charcuterie board with cheese and crackers.

1. In a medium bowl, whisk together 1⅓ cups Blue Plate Mayonnaise, 2 tablespoons whole milk, 2 tablespoons Creole mustard, and 2 teaspoons Louisiana-style hot sauce. Cover and refrigerate until ready to serve.

MAYO-MUSTARD SAUCE

GARLIC ALIOLI

HERB ALIOLI

CONTRIBUTOR

Anthony (Tony) Hietbrink
Co-owner
Bourrée and Boucherie

New Orleans, LA

Anthony Hietbrink is a Flint, Michigan native who has called New Orleans home for more than a decade. In 2023, he became co-owner of Bourrée and Boucherie restaurants, drawing on more than two decades of hospitality experience built largely in front-of-house roles. His one venture into the kitchen was a part-time position as garde manager at Boucherie, where he trained under Chef Nathanial Zimet—now his business partner. That experience left a mark. Anthony's approach to food is grounded in curiosity and creativity, with a particular interest in making familiar flavors feel new. His Fried Chicken Mayo recipe is a direct expression of that instinct—a playful twist on two Southern favorites.

Fried Chicken Mayo

Makes about 2½ cups

You can now create this popular offering from New Orleans' Bourrée at home—and it is much more approachable than you might think. Fried, chopped chicken skins and nanami togarashi, a Japanese seven-spice blend that brings complex, aromatic heat, make this burger and fries sauce surprising as well as irresistibly delicious.

1½ cups Blue Plate Mayonnaise
1 cup Fried Chicken Skins (recipe follows)
2 tablespoons fresh orange juice
1½ tablespoons fresh lime juice
1 tablespoon nanami togarashi, plus more to taste
1½ teaspoons soy sauce
1½ teaspoons onion powder
1 teaspoon garlic powder
¾ teaspoon celery seed
½ teaspoon Cajun seasoning
Salt and ground black pepper, to taste

1. In a medium bowl, whisk together mayonnaise, Fried Chicken Skins, orange juice, lime juice, 1 tablespoon nanami togarashi, soy sauce, onion powder, garlic powder, celery seed, and Cajun seasoning. Season with salt, pepper, and nanami togarashi to taste. Store in an airtight container in the refrigerator for up to 5 days.

Fried Chicken Skins

Makes about 1 cup

Vegetable oil, for frying
4 to 6 breast-sized chicken skins
1 large egg
1 cup Louisiana chicken fry

1. In a medium Dutch oven, heat 2 inches of vegetable oil to 350°F using a deep-frying thermometer.
2. Pat chicken skins dry using paper towels. Lightly beat egg in a shallow dish, and place chicken fry in another. Dredge chicken skins in chicken fry, dip in egg wash, and then dredge again in chicken fry.
3. Fry until golden brown and crisp, 3 to 5 minutes, turning occasionally. Remove and drain on a paper towel–lined baking sheet. Let cool completely. Chop or crush into small, bacon bit–sized pieces.

Crawfish boils start popping up in backyards when the season (from February through May) hits. Affectionately called mudbugs, these freshwater shellfish are available by the sack and can feed a crowd. Make the most of the season and buy extra tail meat to keep in the freezer for crawfish braids at parties (see page 148).

Creamy Deviled Egg Vinaigrette

Makes about 1 cup

Take all the flavors of the perfect deviled egg—rich yolk, creamy consistency, zippy mustard and vinegar—and transform them into a pourable mayo-based dressing. Serve it over composed salads, blanched asparagus, or anywhere you want a unique and rich alternative to everyday dressing.

1. In a medium bowl, combine ⅓ cup cane vinegar and 1 tablespoon minced shallot. Let stand at least 15 minutes.
2. In a small bowl, whisk together ⅓ cup Blue Plate Mayonnaise, ¼ cup Dijon mustard, and 2 large soft-boiled egg yolks until smooth. Add yolk mixture to shallot mixture, whisking to combine. Add 1 tablespoon chopped fresh chives, 1 tablespoon chopped fresh dill, 1½ teaspoons granulated sugar, ¾ teaspoon kosher salt, ½ teaspoon ground black pepper, and ⅛ teaspoon cayenne pepper, whisking to combine. Whisking constantly, gradually add ½ cup extra-virgin olive oil until smooth. Cover and refrigerate for at least 2 hours. Store in an airtight container in refrigerator for up to 3 days.

Cajun Ranch

Makes about 1½ cups

Ranch, Louisiana style, gets heat and spice from a Cajun spice blend, paprika, and hot sauce. Use it as a dressing for pasta salads and slaws, or set it out as a chip dip. Pick your favorite store-bought Cajun seasoning. Those blends tend to include salt in just the right amounts for this dressing, so no additional salt is needed.

1. In a large bowl, whisk together 1 cup Blue Plate Mayonnaise, ½ cup whole buttermilk, 2 teaspoons minced fresh chives, 2 teaspoons minced fresh parsley, 1½ teaspoons minced fresh dill, 1 teaspoon Cajun seasoning, 1 teaspoon white vinegar, 1 teaspoon Louisiana-style hot sauce, ¾ teaspoons paprika, ½ teaspoon garlic powder, and ⅛ teaspoon cayenne pepper until well combined. Use immediately or store in an airtight container in refrigerator for up to 1 week.

Creole Caesar Dressing

Makes about 1 cup

Caesar dressing, a regional staple since the mid-20th century with Italian-American roots, is a natural fit for refreshing garden salads (see Spring Vegetable Salad on page 203), a classic romaine wedge, grilled chicken salad, and more. This version pulls in Creole mustard and anchovy paste to complement the lemony taste.

1. In a small bowl, whisk together 1 cup Blue Plate Mayonnaise, 2 tablespoons fresh lemon juice, 4 teaspoons anchovy paste, 4 teaspoons Worcestershire sauce, 4 teaspoons Creole mustard, 1 teaspoon kosher salt, ½ teaspoon ground black pepper, and 4 minced cloves garlic until well combined. Refrigerate until ready to serve. Store in an airtight container in refrigerator for up to 1 week.

Green Goddess Dressing

Makes about 2 cups

This Blue Plate Mayonnaise version of the herb-packed dressing is quick and easy to make with the use of a blender or food processor. Avocado, fresh parsley, chives, and tarragon create the dressing's dramatic pale green color. Anchovy paste lends salty umami depth, without adding fishy taste. Green Goddess Dressing has California cuisine roots but fits in beautifully with Gulf Coast and Delta Region foodways, from fried green tomatoes to a crisp garden salad to grilled shrimp.

1. In the bowl of a food processor, pulse together 1 cup Blue Plate Mayonnaise; ½ cup sour cream or plain low-fat yogurt; ½ cup fresh parsley leaves; ¼ cup chopped fresh chives; 2 tablespoons chopped fresh tarragon; 2 tablespoons fresh lemon juice; ½ teaspoon anchovy paste; ½ teaspoon kosher salt; ½ teaspoon ground black pepper; 1 peeled, pitted, and chopped avocado; and 1 clove garlic until smooth. Transfer to a resealable jar, and refrigerate until ready to serve. Refrigerate remaining dressing for up to 1 week.

CREAMY
COCKTAIL
SAUCE
TARTAR
SAUCE

Creamy Cocktail Sauce

Makes about 1¼ cups

Everyday cocktail sauce gets an elegant upgrade with the addition of mayonnaise and brings velvety richness to shrimp cocktail, crab claws, and more. This innovative spin offers a unique alternative to the classic, mellowing the acidic nature of the ketchup and sharp bite that horseradish brings into something smoother and more indulgent. Try it also as a surprise ingredient stirred into potato salad.

1. In a medium bowl, whisk together ¾ cup Blue Plate Mayonnaise and 3 tablespoons ketchup until smooth. Add 2 tablespoons prepared horseradish, 1 tablespoon fresh lemon juice, 1 teaspoon Worcestershire sauce, ½ teaspoon kosher salt, ½ teaspoon paprika, ¼ teaspoon onion powder, ¼ teaspoon garlic powder, and ¼ teaspoon ground black pepper, stirring with a whisk until fully combined.
2. Transfer sauce to an airtight container, and refrigerate at least 30 minutes before serving; this helps meld the flavors. Store in an airtight container, and refrigerate for up to 3 days.

Tartar Sauce

Makes about 1½ cups

Pickle fans, this one's for you. Cornichons bring a mix of tart and sweet to this tartar sauce, a regular you will encounter with every fried seafood platter. Balancing the tangy with the rich and creamy is crucial, and this recipe gets it just right, making it the perfect seafood sauce to have on hand.

1. In a small bowl, whisk together 1½ cups Blue Plate Mayonnaise, 2 tablespoons finely chopped sweet onion, 2 tablespoons finely chopped cornichons, 1 tablespoon minced shallot, 1 tablespoon minced garlic, ½ teaspoon lemon zest, 1 tablespoon fresh lemon juice, 2 teaspoons chopped fresh parsley, ½ teaspoon salt, and ¼ teaspoon cayenne pepper until well combined. Cover and refrigerate for at least 1 hour before serving. The sauce can be made and stored in the refrigerator up to 4 days in advance.

Shortcut Hollandaise

Makes about 1½ cups

Hollandaise, a butter and egg yolk emulsion, is one of five French mother sauces (a recipe that others can be built from), and for anyone short on time or slightly fearful of getting it wrong, this recipe is the way to go. Egg yolk–based mayonnaise lets you skip the painstaking process of carefully blending the two ingredients without the mixture breaking (a cheffy word for separating). Melted butter is whisked in at the end to achieve that signature buttery flavor. Creole mustard and smoked paprika give this version a Louisiana personality, though traditionalists can omit them and substitute a little Dijon mustard in their place. A complete reward with very little effort and a way to get eggs Benedict, stuffed artichokes, or poached fish to the table fast.

1. Melt ¼ cup unsalted butter in a small bowl. Let cool.
2. In a medium bowl, whisk together 1 cup Blue Plate Mayonnaise, 1 teaspoon fresh lemon juice, 1 teaspoon Creole mustard, and ¼ teaspoon smoked paprika. Whisk in cooled butter, 1 tablespoon at a time, until well combined. Stir in 1 teaspoon Louisiana-style hot sauce, if desired, and season with salt to taste.

Bearnaise Sauce

Makes about 1½ cups

As with Hollandaise, Bearnaise Sauce starts with an egg yolk and butter emulsion. It's finished with tarragon, shallots, and a splash of white wine and is traditionally served with steak. This shortcut version uses mayonnaise as its base to deliver all the richness without the technical risk.

1. Melt ¼ cup unsalted butter in a medium bowl. Let cool slightly.
2. Add 1 cup Blue Plate Mayonnaise, 3 tablespoons chopped fresh tarragon, 2 tablespoons dry white wine, ½ teaspoon lemon zest, 1 tablespoon fresh lemon juice, 1 teaspoon Dijon mustard, 1 teaspoon finely chopped shallot, and ½ teaspoon finely chopped garlic to butter, stirring with a whisk to combine.

SHORTCUT HOLLANDAISE

CHAPTER 8

Save Some Room

From cornbread and pound cakes to cookies, waffles, biscuits, and cobblers, baking is an integral part of daily life across the Gulf South. Whether created to enjoy for celebrations, just a little something after dinner, or with an afternoon cup of coffee, these recipes sweeten the day. Along the way, you'll find mayonnaise in some unexpected places and discover that Blue Plate's egg yolk base brings essential magic to the table.

Banana Bread

Makes 1 (9x5-inch) loaf

A church potluck and Sunday supper fixture, banana bread was born out of a thrifty way to use up overripe bananas, the advent of baking powder and baking soda for the home cook, and the economic realities of the Great Depression. This recipe innovates with mayonnaise which replaces the fats, commonly butter or oil, and also contributes to the binding power supplied by the eggs. This quick bread loaf emerges from the oven extremely moist with the perfect level of sweetness. Make sure to use very ripe bananas for the best flavor and easier mashing and mixing. The recipe calls for dark chocolate, but you can also use bittersweet. Avoid milk chocolate—it is too sweet for this recipe.

- **1½ cups mashed ripe banana (3 to 4 large bananas)**
- **1 cup Blue Plate Mayonnaise**
- **1 cup granulated sugar**
- **1 teaspoon vanilla extract**
- **1 large egg, lightly beaten**
- **1½ cups all-purpose flour**
- **2 teaspoons baking powder**
- **½ teaspoon kosher salt**
- **¾ cup coarsely chopped pecans**
- **¾ cup dark chocolate chunks**

1. Preheat oven to 350°F. Spray a 9x5-inch loaf pan with cooking spray. Line with parchment paper so that the parchment hangs over all four sides.

2. In a large bowl, whisk together mashed banana, mayonnaise, sugar, vanilla, and egg until well combined.

3. In a medium bowl, whisk together flour, baking powder, and salt. Fold dry ingredients, pecans, and chocolate chunks into banana mixture just until no streaks of flour can be seen. Pour batter into prepared pan.

4. Bake until a wooden pick inserted into the center comes out clean, 1 hour to 1 hour and 10 minutes. Cool in pan on a wire rack 15 minutes, then remove from pan. Cool completely, then wrap tightly in foil and store in an airtight container. It keeps well at room temperature up to 5 days, and it also freezes well.

WHAT IS A QUICK BREAD? A quick bread is made with leaveners, such as baking powder and baking soda rather than yeast. In the South, where kitchens were often hot and time was short, quick breads offered a practical alternative to yeast breads. The key, as with muffins, is to not overmix the batter once the flour is added to avoid developing the flour's gluten and producing a rubbery, tough crumb. Fold in the dry ingredients only until it is just incorporated.

CLASSIC
DROP
BISCUITS
GARLIC AND CHIVE
DROP BISCUITS

DROP BISCUITS 3 WAYS

Classic Drop Biscuits

Makes 12 to 16

Breakfast, lunch, dinner, and all the nibbles in between are a welcome setting for these drop biscuits. They're a quick and easy alternative to rolled and cut butter biscuits and rely on self-rising flour and mayonnaise as helpful time-savers. Mayonnaise is the fat replacement in the mix and circumvents the need to cut in cold cubes of butter. It also gives the biscuits their golden crowns, behaving in the same way as brushing an egg wash or cream on the tops before baking to encourage browning. They are great made plain and served with jam or ham or to sop up gravy. Or try one of the variations: Garlic and Chive Drop Biscuits, a savory option, pair well with most dinners, and Cinnamon Sugar Drop Biscuits make a great breakfast offering or afternoon snack.

- ⅔ **cup whole milk**
- ½ **cup plus 1 tablespoon Blue Plate Mayonnaise, divided**
- 2 **cups self-rising flour (see Note)**
- 2 **teaspoons water**

1. Preheat oven to 425°F. Line a large rimmed baking sheet with parchment paper.

2. In a large bowl, whisk together milk and ½ cup mayonnaise. Add flour, and stir just until combined.

3. Drop about 2 tablespoons batter at a time onto the prepared baking sheet, about 2 inches apart. In a small bowl, whisk together remaining 1 tablespoon mayonnaise and 2 teaspoons water. Brush mayonnaise mixture onto biscuits.

4. Bake until golden, 12 to 15 minutes. Serve warm. Wrap leftovers in plastic wrap or store in an airtight container at room temperature for up to 2 days.

Note: If you don't have self-rising flour, substitute 2 cups all-purpose flour plus 1 tablespoon baking powder and 1 teaspoon kosher salt.

Garlic and Chive Drop Biscuits

Make biscuits as directed, adding 2 tablespoons finely chopped fresh chives and 1 teaspoon garlic powder to the batter.

Cinnamon Sugar Drop Biscuits

Make biscuits as directed, adding 3 tablespoons granulated sugar to the batter. Whisk together 2 tablespoons granulated sugar and ½ teaspoon ground cinnamon, and sprinkle over the top of the biscuits before baking.

In the early 1800s, Haitian refugees brought their building skills and style to New Orleans: shotgun houses, long and narrow homes one room wide and two or three rooms deep. Recognized as a significant African American architectural contribution, the style first took hold in the city's Bywater and Marigny neighborhoods. After the Civil War, shotgun houses spread across the Gulf South, from Mobile's Down the Bay neighborhood to Houston's Third Ward and beyond. Throughout the 19th century, homeowners decorated the houses with gingerbread-style trim and vibrant paint colors. They remain an iconic symbol of New Orleans and the Gulf South's coastal cities.

Photo by Ryan Hodgson-Rigsbee

Waffles

Makes about 8

For crispy waffles with tender, pillowy interiors, this recipe skips the eggs and instead employs mayonnaise in the batter. That fat helps the exterior fry to a golden brown with the sugar in the batter and the mayo aiding the caramelization. Even the moisture in the mayonnaise plays a part, creating steam that gives the waffles their airy, light texture. If you're making waffles for a crowd, keep the ones coming out of the waffle maker warm by placing them in a single layer on a wire rack in a rimmed baking sheet in a low-temperature oven (around 200°F.) while you work. Serve the waffles with butter and cane or maple syrup and topped with fresh berries or as a dessert with vanilla ice cream, warm caramel sauce, and praline pecans. Or go the savory route and offer them with fried chicken and a drizzle of hot honey.

2 cups all-purpose flour
1 tablespoon baking powder
2 teaspoons granulated sugar
½ teaspoon kosher salt
1½ cups whole milk
½ cup Blue Plate Mayonnaise
¼ cup unsalted butter, melted and cooled slightly
Butter and cane syrup or maple syrup, to serve

1. In a large bowl, whisk together flour, baking powder, sugar, and salt. Add milk, mayonnaise, and melted butter, whisking until combined.
2. Heat waffle maker to manufacturer's instructions. Lightly spray with cooking spray.
3. Spoon ½ cup batter into waffle maker. Cook according to manufacturer's instructions until golden brown. Continue with remaining batter, spraying with cooking spray between batches as needed. Serve warm with butter and syrup.

Skillet Cornbread

Makes 1 (10-inch) loaf

When you pour cornbread batter into a hot cast-iron skillet where oil sizzles ready to do its work frying the bottom to a deep golden brown while the interior bakes, you know you're in for something special. Combined with buttermilk, mayonnaise contributes richness to this cornbread and helps create a moist, tender crumb. Southern cornbread is the topic of regional debate when it comes to several things: yellow or white cornmeal, the size of the meal grind, and the most polarizing subject—whether sweetener of any kind belongs in the batter. This recipe includes a touch of cane syrup that brings subtle caramel notes and deepens the flavor more than it sweetens, but, if you wish, you can omit the syrup.

1 tablespoon olive oil
2 cups finely ground yellow cornmeal
1 cup all-purpose flour
1 teaspoon baking powder
¾ teaspoon kosher salt
½ teaspoon baking soda
⅛ teaspoon cayenne pepper (optional)
1½ cups whole buttermilk
¾ cup Blue Plate Mayonnaise
1 large egg, room temperature
2 tablespoons cane syrup, plus more for serving
2 tablespoons butter, melted
Butter, to serve

1. Preheat oven to 400°F. Place oil in a 10-inch cast-iron or other heavy, ovenproof skillet, and transfer to oven to preheat.
2. In a large bowl, whisk together cornmeal, flour, baking powder, salt, baking soda, and cayenne, if desired, until well combined.
3. In a separate bowl, whisk together buttermilk, mayonnaise, egg, and cane syrup. Combine wet and dry ingredients, stirring to mix well.
4. Carefully remove the hot skillet from the oven. Pour batter into skillet, and bake until a wooden pick inserted in the center comes out clean, 20 to 25 minutes.
5. Pour melted butter over the cornbread as soon as it comes out of the oven. Let stand for 5 to 10 minutes before serving with butter and cane syrup.

CANE SYRUP, a sweetener cooks rely on throughout the Gulf South, is made from juicing sugarcane and reducing it into a syrup. A cousin to molasses, it too offers caramel notes, but with a lighter, cleaner taste. Louisianians favor Steen's Pure Cane Syrup, recognizable by its familiar yellow can. Throughout the Gulf Coast, it has long been preferred as a drizzle over biscuits, a sweetener for baked goods, and a way to add subtle sweetness and depth to savory dishes.

"Our Daily Bread"
Asbury United Methodist
"The Church With A Friendly Heart"
101 Five Oak Blvd.
Acadian Bi-Centennial
Cooking with Friends
presented by
The St. Martin Parish Council on Aging
DON'S SECRETS
providing
COOKING MAGIC FOR OUR RESTAURANTS IN
LAFAYETTE
BATON ROUGE
SHREVEPORT
HAMMOND
BEAUMONT
CORN MEAL ROLLS
HOME-MADE ROLLS
HOT ROLLS
Book 1
Cajun / Creole Family Album
New Orleans
CHEFS' CHARITY FOR CHILDREN
2015
Paintings by George Rodrigue
SEAFOOD
206 Meats, etc.
BASIC RED SAUCE
POULTRY
Manna from Asbury
compiled by
The United Methodist Women
of
Asbury United Methodist Church
Justin Wilson
COOK BOOK

Crabs & Lobsters
BOILED LOBSTER
Maria Bertucci Compagno's
Sicilian-Style Cooking
From Usitca to New Orleans
Compagno's Restaurant 1929-1998
CAJUN CUISINE
Authentic Cajun Recipes From Louisiana's Bayous
Tree-Trimming Party
Warm-Ups for Carolers
Recipes for America's Mixed Drink Revolution
OPEN HOUSE PUNCH
SCARLETT O'HARA
HOT BUTTERED COMFORT
k About Good II
Le Livre de Cuisine des Acadiens
& FEASTS
& Shirley Dauterive Angelle
THE ANGELLE FAMILY Cookbook
VEGETABLES
RED BEANS AND SAUSAGE
SWEET POTATO SOUFFLÉ
D. LANDRY'S SWEET POTATO CAS
favorite RECIPES from FAMOUS NEW ORLEANS RESTAURANTS
VOILÀ!
Lafayette Centennial Cookbook 1884 1984
A Century of Acadiana Cooking from Open Fire to Microwave
Jean K Durkee
Swamp Dynasty Lagniappe
Louisiana LEGACY

Lemon Pound Cake

Makes 1 (10-cup) cake

Bring this Lemon Pound Cake, baked in a Bundt pan and crowned with an opaque lemon glaze that drips dramatically down the sides, to the table and stand back for the oohs and aahs. Named for the way home cooks could easily memorize the recipe (a pound each of the main ingredients), traditional pound cake has long been a staple of Southern celebrations and gatherings. Where this cake differs from traditional recipes is that, instead of butter, Blue Plate Mayonnaise is the fat that enriches it (see Note). That switch also makes mixing the batter remarkably simple. There's no butter to cream and no special technique required, just a straightforward batter that bakes into a rich, tender cake with the dense, moist crumb pound cake lovers expect.

1⅔ cups granulated sugar
1 tablespoon lemon zest
1 cup Blue Plate Mayonnaise
2½ tablespoons fresh lemon juice, divided
1½ teaspoons vanilla extract
2 large eggs, room temperature
2½ cups all-purpose flour
2½ teaspoons baking powder
¼ teaspoon kosher salt
⅔ cup whole milk, room temperature
1 cup confectioners' sugar

1. Preheat oven to 350°F. Lightly spray a 10-cup Bundt pan with baking spray with flour (see Note).

2. In a large bowl, whisk together granulated sugar and lemon zest until fragrant, about 1 minute. Add mayonnaise, 1 tablespoon lemon juice, vanilla, and eggs, and whisk until smooth and combined.

3. In a medium bowl, whisk together flour, baking powder, and salt. Gradually add flour mixture to sugar mixture, alternating with the milk, whisking until just combined after each addition. Pour batter into prepared pan.

4. Bake until a wooden pick inserted near the center comes out clean, 45 to 50 minutes. Let cool in pan for 10 minutes, then move cake to a wire rack to cool completely.

5. In a small bowl, whisk together confectioners' sugar and remaining 1½ tablespoons lemon juice. Pour over cooled cake.

Note: The pound cake can also be baked in a 9x5-inch loaf pan. Spray the pan with baking spray and line with parchment paper so that it hangs over all four sides. Prepare batter as directed. Bake until a wooden pick inserted in the center comes out clean, 1 hour 5 minutes to 1 hour 10 minutes. Continue with glaze as directed.

Chocolate-Coffee Layer Cake

Makes 1 (9-inch) cake

Most home bakers know all about the "trick" of using mayonnaise to make a chocolate cake and for good reason: It works. Mayonnaise supplies the fat that gives this cake its rich flavor, moisture, and tenderness. This modern version pairs deep chocolate flavor with dark roast coffee and is frosted with melt-in-your-mouth Creamy Chocolate Frosting. Brown sugar, with its molasses notes, takes the place of granulated sugar and intensifies the chocolate experience. Frost the cake only after the layers have completely cooled. For a picture-perfect look, trim the tops of the layers to level them, and flip the top layer, cut side down, to apply the frosting evenly and with far less crumbs. Serve slices of this cake with vanilla ice cream and a robust cup of coffee. This is the kind of cake that belongs at birthdays, graduations, and other celebrations worthy of a fantastic chocolate cake.

1⅓ cups hot dark roast coffee
¾ cup unsweetened cocoa powder
2½ cups Swans Down Cake Flour
1¼ teaspoons baking soda
½ teaspoon kosher salt
¼ teaspoon baking powder
1⅔ cups firmly packed light brown sugar
3 large eggs, room temperature
1 cup Blue Plate Mayonnaise, room temperature
Creamy Chocolate Frosting (page 241)

1. Preheat oven to 325°F. Spray 2 (9-inch) round cake pans with baking spray and line bottoms with parchment paper.
2. Whisk together hot coffee and cocoa powder in a 2-cup glass measuring cup until completely blended. Let stand until cooled.
3. In a large bowl, sift together flour, baking soda, salt, and baking powder; set aside. In another large bowl, combine brown sugar and eggs, and beat with a mixer at high speed until light and fluffy, about 3 minutes, stopping to scrape sides of bowl. Add mayonnaise, and beat at low speed until well combined. Gradually add flour mixture alternately with coffee mixture, beginning and ending with flour mixture, beating just until combined after each addition.
4. Divide batter between prepared pans. Bake until a wooden pick inserted in center comes out clean, 30 to 35 minutes. Let cool in pans 10 minutes. Remove from pans onto wire racks, and let cool completely. Level cake layers, if desired; remove and discard parchment.
5. Spread Creamy Chocolate Frosting between layers and on top and sides of cake.

Creamy Chocolate Frosting

Makes about 5½ cups

This silky-smooth chocolate frosting gets its luxurious consistency from mayonnaise. Butter brings flavor, while the mayonnaise allows the frosting to whip into a luscious texture that spreads beautifully over cakes and cupcakes. Unsweetened cocoa powder provides concentrated chocolate flavor and a rich, beautiful color. The frosting can be made up to 2 days ahead and refrigerated. Let it come to room temperature and beat briefly before using to restore its smooth, spreadable texture.

- 1 **cup unsalted butter, softened**
- 1 **cup Blue Plate Mayonnaise, room temperature**
- ½ **teaspoon kosher salt**
- 5 **cups confectioners' sugar**
- 1 **cup unsweetened cocoa powder**
- 2 **tablespoons heavy whipping cream**
- ½ **teaspoon vanilla extract**

1. In the bowl of a stand mixer fitted with the paddle attachment, beat butter, mayonnaise, and salt at low speed until smooth.
2. In a large bowl, sift together confectioners' sugar and cocoa. Slowly add sugar mixture, about 1 cup at a time, to butter mixture alternately with cream, about 1 teaspoon at a time, beating until smooth after each addition. Beat in vanilla. Increase mixer speed to medium, and beat until fluffy, 2 to 3 minutes.

Whipped Vanilla Frosting

Makes about 5 cups

Fluffy and light and white as snow, Whipped Vanilla Frosting is the cupcake topper, cookie filling, and finishing touch for the bake-sale treats you need to keep in your back pocket. It evokes childhood memories of snack cakes and coconut-covered layer cakes and comes together effortlessly with just a mixer and a bowl. Let the kids lick the beaters or save them for yourself. You'll want to enjoy every last swipe of this sweet treat.

- 1¼ **cups unsalted butter, softened**
- 8 **cups confectioners' sugar, sifted**
- ¾ **cup Blue Plate Mayonnaise, room temperature**
- 1½ **teaspoons vanilla extract**
- ¼ **teaspoon kosher salt**

1. In the bowl of a stand mixer fitted with a paddle attachment, beat butter at medium speed until soft and creamy, 1 to 2 minutes. Reduce mixer speed to low. Beat in confectioners' sugar, 2 cups at a time, alternating with mayonnaise, 2 tablespoons at a time, until well combined. Add in vanilla and salt. Beat until well combined. Increase mixer speed to medium high, and beat until frosting is fluffy, 2 to 3 minutes.

CONTRIBUTOR

Cheryl Slocum
Writer, Editor, and
Recipe Developer

Birmingham, AL

Cheryl Slocum loves telling food stories and has helped shape some of the nation's most influential food and lifestyle publications, including *Food & Wine, Country Living*, and *Cooking Light*. Her Hudson Valley, New York, memories of food and cooking have informed her love of baking, while her years of calling Alabama home have deepened her appreciation for Southern foodways. Drawn to nostalgic American desserts, Slocum embraces old-fashioned cakes, from angel food to pound cake, and remains inspired by the holiday baking days of her childhood, when Christmas cookies and Thanksgiving pies brought family together in the kitchen.

Spiced Sandwich Cookies

Makes 14

These cookies are infused with warm spices and get a mild nuttiness from toasted pecans that are ground into a smooth nut butter with the assistance of mayonnaise. Cinnamon, ginger, nutmeg, and allspice give the cookies a flavor reminiscent of gingerbread. Little mounds of dough are gently pressed to create the sandwich halves which are filled with Whipped Vanilla Frosting (page 241) that gets a bright boost from lemon zest.

- 1¾ **cups cake flour**
- 1½ **teaspoons ground cinnamon**
- 1½ **teaspoons ground ginger**
- ¾ **teaspoon salt**
- ½ **teaspoon nutmeg, preferably freshly grated**
- ¼ **teaspoon allspice**
- 1 **cup toasted pecan halves**
- ½ **cup Blue Plate Mayonnaise**
- ¼ **cup unsalted butter, softened**
- ¾ **cup packed light brown sugar**
- ¼ **cup granulated sugar**
- 1 **teaspoon vanilla extract**
- 1 **large egg**
- **Zest of 1 large lemon**
- ½ **recipe Whipped Vanilla Frosting (page 241)**

1. Preheat oven to 375°F. Line a large baking sheet with parchment paper.
2. In a medium bowl, whisk together cake flour, cinnamon, ginger, salt, nutmeg, and allspice in a bowl; set aside.
3. Place pecans and mayonnaise in the work bowl of a food processor; process until smooth and loose, like a pourable nut butter with no visible pecan pieces remaining.
4. Using an electric hand mixer on medium-low speed, beat pecan butter, softened butter, brown sugar, granulated sugar, and vanilla together until well combined. Beat in egg until the mixture is smooth and glossy.
5. Stir flour mixture into pecan butter mixture until just combined. Dough will be thick, soft, and slightly glossy—closer to a thick batter than a stiff cookie dough.
6. Drop 1 tablespoon dough per cookie on prepared pan. Flatten each mound with lightly floured fingers to an even ¼-inch thickness, about 2 inches in diameter.
7. Bake until cookies are set and golden on the bottom, 10 to 12 minutes. Cool completely before filling.
8. Using an electric hand mixer on medium-low speed, beat lemon zest into Whipped Vanilla Frosting until fluffy. Spread about 1½ to 2 tablespoons filling on the flat side of 1 cookie and sandwich with another cookie. Repeat with remaining cookies and frosting.

At dusk, roseate spoonbills, their silhouettes traced against a dramatic Southern sky, roost in the branches of cypress trees growing in coastal wetlands. By day, they wade through the shallow marshes to feed on small fish and crustaceans.

Peach Cobbler

Makes 10 to 12 servings

Peach cobbler lands on almost every Southern table when stone fruit is in season. This recipe is for a batter-topped cobbler (rather than biscuits) that bakes to a cakelike texture with a delicately crusty, golden top. When the fruit is ripe and at its peak, you can reduce the sugar in the filling, but the simple-to-mix topping has just the right amount of sweetness and gets an assist from mayonnaise, which helps create a tender crumb. Serve warm or at room temperature with a scoop of vanilla ice cream for a cool, creamy contrast.

Filling

½ cup granulated sugar
¼ cup firmly packed light brown sugar
¼ cup cornstarch
1 teaspoon ground cinnamon
½ teaspoon kosher salt
½ teaspoon ground nutmeg
6 cups fresh or frozen sliced peaches

Topping

1½ cups all-purpose flour
1½ teaspoons baking powder
¼ teaspoon kosher salt
1½ cups granulated sugar
⅓ cup Blue Plate Mayonnaise
⅓ cup whole buttermilk, room temperature
2 large eggs, room temperature
Vanilla Bean Ice Cream (page 248)

1. Preheat oven to 375°F. Lightly spray a 13x9-inch glass baking dish with cooking spray.
2. Make the filling: In a large bowl, whisk together sugars, cornstarch, cinnamon, salt, and nutmeg. Add peaches, and toss to coat. Pour into prepared baking pan.
3. Make the topping: In a medium bowl, whisk together flour, baking powder, and salt.
4. In another large bowl, whisk together granulated sugar, mayonnaise, and buttermilk until well combined. Whisk in eggs. Add flour mixture to mayonnaise mixture, stirring just until combined; spoon on top of peaches.
5. Bake until lightly golden and set on top, 55 minutes to 1 hour. Serve warm with Vanilla Bean Ice Cream.

Vanilla Bean Ice Cream

Makes about 4 cups

Making traditional homemade ice cream can feel daunting, with the tempering of egg yolks and cooking required to create a custard base. In this recipe, Blue Plate Mayonnaise, already an egg yolk-based emulsion and high in fat, eliminates the need for cooked custard altogether. The result is a silky, rich ice cream flecked with vanilla that is surprisingly easy to make. The base simply needs to be well chilled before churning. And since there is no hot custard to cool, everything comes together faster and with far less fuss. Serve this ice cream in a sugar cone, formed with cake layers into an ice cream cake, or melting over a warm serving of Peach Cobbler (page 247).

- ¾ **cup granulated sugar**
- ¼ **cup Blue Plate Mayonnaise**
- 2 **cups heavy whipping cream**
- ½ **cup whole milk**
- 1 **tablespoon vanilla bean paste**

1. In a medium bowl, whisk together sugar and mayonnaise until smooth and combined. Add cream, milk, and vanilla bean paste, whisking until combined. Cover and refrigerate for at least 8 hours.
2. Churn mixture in an ice-cream maker according to manufacturer's instructions. Serve immediately for soft serve or freeze in an airtight container for a firmer ice cream texture, at least 3 hours.

Photo by Ryan Hodgson-Rigsbee

THANK YOU

To the photographers, writers, editors, designers, chefs, home cooks, and everyone who lent their talents, stories, and time to these pages.

To Cheryl Slocum, for giving a voice to the stories, traditions, and spirit that shape this region.

To Denny Culbert, for capturing the beauty and warmth of the Gulf South.

To the team at 83 Press, for your steady guidance in bringing this book to life.

To Kelly Huling, Matt Dugas, and Brad Brewster at Relevant Studios, for your creativity and care in shaping every page.

To Hannah Jobe, Dan Trahant, and John Koerner at Reily Foods Company, for championing *Dressed*, shaping its vision, and stewarding it from its earliest idea to these pages.

To the Reily Family for keeping Blue Plate family made and carrying forward a legacy built around good food and good company.

Dressed is just a glimpse of the people, places, and traditions that continue to define the Gulf South. It has been our privilege to tell a small part of that story.

Index

T

V

W

Sabiene Autsch

Micro Archives

Arbeiten 2018–2024

Texte/Texts

Edition Imorde
Berlin 2024

Gestaltung: Troppo Design
Gesamtherstellung:
Thomas Dehne, dehne-druck.de
Printed in Germany
ISBN 123-123-123

Jens Schröter

Die Serien des Sichtbaren

«Künftig ist das Problem das der Konstituierung von Serien» bemerkte Michel Foucault 1969 in seiner *Archäologie des Wissens*.[1] Dieses Problems nimmt sich Sabiene Autsch in ihrer künstlerisch-kuratorischen Arbeit an und verbindet sie auf originelle Weise mit den Operationen des Archivs. Der Katalog oder die Ausstellung ist das Archiv von Sabiene Autschs Fotografien – diese bilden Natur, Städte, aber auch von ihr angefertigte Collagen ab. Sabiene Autsch konstelliert die Bilder zu Serien. Wie der Kunsthistoriker Benjamin Buchloh bemerkt, ist diese «Heterogenität des Bildmaterials» typisch für viele klassische Strategien der Montage – und diese Heterogenität wurde einerseits, etwa im Dadaismus als «potentiell revolutionärer Schockeffekt» eingesetzt, andererseits befürchteten die Dadaisten aber auch die «depolitisierende Wirkung einer affirmativen, jegliche Möglichkeit sozialer Verständigung ausschließende […] Zusammenhanglosigkeit.» Daraus sei, so Buchloh, das «Epistem der archivalischen Ordnung»[2] hervorgegangen: Eine «Sammlung von Einzelfotos, die erst in ihrer Gesamtheit einen akkumulativen, mehr oder minder kohärenten Einblick in die Komplexität eines gegebenen Sujets erlauben.»[3] Allerdings nutzt Sabiene Autsch einerseits kein gefundenes Bildmaterial, sondern eigene Fotos (die wiederum gefundenes Bildmaterial in collagierter Form enthalten können). Andererseits geht es mitnichten um einen «Einblick» in ein «gegebenes Sujet», sondern vielmehr um die Bildung von formalen Serien, die die einzelnen Bilder auf verschiedene Weise verbinden und transversal durchqueren. Das «Sujet» ist daher nicht auf der Ebene des Inhalts, sondern auf jenem der Form angesiedelt. Die Bilder sind nicht durch eine Ikonographie verbunden (wie Buchloh es bei Broodthaers absurden Ansammlungen zum Thema «Adler» beschreibt), noch durch eine iterative Permutation, wie in den Fotografien industriekultureller Objekte von Bernd und Hilla Becher. Hier wird ein anderes Epistem archivalischer Ordnung erprobt, das die Bilder *als Bilder* und nicht als Zeichen, die ikonisch und indexikalisch auf realweltliche Vorkommnisse verweisen, ernstnimmt. Die hier erprobte «archivalische Ordnung» begründet ein Archiv formaler Serien, die Bilder von Sabiene Autsch aus verschiedenen Zeiträumen und Orten verbindet. Aber, so könnte man kritisch einwenden: Ist das nicht ein Rückfall in eine Hypostase auktorialer Subjektivität? Unterminiert die ausschließliche Nutzung eigener Bilder (statt vorgefundenen Bildmaterials) nicht gerade den «‹Antisubjektivismus› als einer treibenden Kraft der Collage-Ästhetik.»[4] Sicher, das auktoriale Subjekt wird bei

1 Foucault, Michel: Archäologie des Wissens. Frankfurt a. M.: Suhrkamp 1981, hier S. 20.
2 Buchloh, Benjamin H. D.: Warburgs Vorbild? Das Ende der Collage/Fotomontage im Nachkriegseuropa, in: Ebeling, Knut; Günzel, Stephan (Hg.): Archivologie. Theorien des Archivs in Wissenschaft, Medien und Künsten. Berlin: Kadmos 2009, S. 233–252, hier S. 240.
3 Ebd., S. 242.
4 Ebd., S. 238.

Sabiene Autsch nicht durch die Montage von heterogenem und vor allem gefundenem Bildmaterial zerstreut. In der Montage sprechen die zitierten Bilder sozusagen mit anderer Stimme und unterlaufen die Kohärenz der Stimme der Autor*in. Aber auch gegenüber gefundenem Bildmaterial bleibt das konstellierende Autor*innensubjekt *als konstellierendes* immer noch in einer Position der strukturierenden Macht. Die Strategie von Sabiene Autsch ist radikaler: Sie betont, dass die Elemente, die die Fotografien und Collagen zu Serien verbinden, nicht in der Produktion der Bilder angelegt sind. Sie werden vielmehr erst sichtbar in der reflektierten Praxis des Konstellierens, d.h. in der An- und Um-Ordnung, in der Zusammenstellung und Ausstellung zum Micro-Archive. D. h. Sabiene Autsch macht Serien sichtbar, die ihr als Autorin der Bilder gar nicht bewusst waren. «Ich sehe mich mich nicht sehen.»[5] Jedes Foto ist eine sehr bewusste Handlung und dennoch schleicht sich etwas ins Bild. Das Unbewusste der Künstlerin erscheint in den Serien und durchquert Bilder aus verschiedenen Zeiten und Orten. Das Unbewusste ist, wie Deleuze argumentiert hat, selbst «differentiell und iterativ, seriell, problematisch und befragend.»[6] Als serielles kann es nur in Serien erscheinen. Das Sujet der Montage ist eben nicht «gegeben», wie Buchloh argumentiert, sondern taucht erst aus der Konstellation der Bilder auf. Es erscheint in der Spannung zwischen den Bildern.

Dieses Unbewusste sollte nicht als Prozess der Verdrängung und des Vergessens traumatischer Erlebnisse verstanden werden. Vielmehr ist es ein Optisch-Unbewusstes[7], eine Struktur, die das Sichtbare zunächst unbemerkt durchzieht: Eine orangefarbene Form in einer Collage – ein Kreis im Steinboden auf einem Foto – eine mittige Tür ähnlicher Farbe ... später taucht ein roter Kreis auf ... Oder: Rasterförmige Strukturen eines Treppengeländers – ebensolche Strukturen in einer Lagerhalle und an einer Promenade ... am Boden eines Schwimmbeckens, in einer Zeichnung, in Licht und Schatten in einem Wald ... Oder: Die Farbe Grün ... ganz verschiedene Bilder, die sich in ihrer Struktur einer Serie verbinden ...

«Erfahrung und Struktur,» so der Titel einer Monografie von Friedrich Kambartel von 1976, als Teil einer Collage, bringt es auf den Punkt: Unsere Erfahrung ist ständig von unbewussten seriellen Strukturen durchformt, die erst in der künstlerischen Konstellation im Micro-Archive der Ausstellung oder des Katalogs sichtbar werden. So verfremdet die Künstlerin den Blick auf Alltägliches. Sie nimmt der Erfahrung jede Schließung und macht ihre Leerstellen sichtbar. Waldenfels hat einmal vorgeschlagen von «einer Bildhaftigkeit in den Dingen zu sprechen, die der Bildhaftigkeit von Bildnissen vorausgeht.»[8] Die Künstlerin konstelliert Bilder, um eben diese ursprüngliche Bildhaftigkeit in den Serien wieder sichtbar zu machen. Hier ist das Ganze mehr als die Summe der Teile. Sabiene Autsch taucht ein in das Sichtbare, ja löst sich geradezu darin auf, um uns dann eine Erfahrung der Struktur zu ermöglichen.

5 Därmann, Iris: Tod und Bild. Eine phänomenologische Mediengeschichte. München: Fink 1995, S. 409.
6 Deleuze, Gilles: Differenz und Wiederholung. München: Fink 1997, S. 144.
7 Vgl. Krauss, Rosalind: The Optical Unconscious. Cambridge/MA: MIT Press 1993.
8 Waldenfels, Bernhard: Spiegel, Spur und Blick. Zur Genese des Bildes, in: Böhm, Gottfried (Hg.): Homo Pictor. München: Saur 2001, S. 14–31, hier S. 20.

Jens Schröter

The Series of the Visible

Michel Foucault remarked in 1969 in his *Archaeology of Knowledge*: «The problem now is to constitute series.»[9] Sabiene Autsch addresses this problem in her artistic-curatorial work and combines it in an original way with the operations of the archive. The catalog or exhibition is the archive of Sabiene Autsch's photographs – these depict nature, cities, but the catalog or exhibition also includes collages made by her. Sabiene Autsch constellates different images into series. As the art historian Benjamin Buchloh notes, this «heterogeneity»[10] is typical of many classic strategies of montage – and this heterogeneity was used on the one hand, for example in Dadaism, as a «potentially revolutionary shock effect», but on the other hand the Dadaists also feared the «‹depoliticizing› effect of an affirmative possibility of social agreement on exclusive discontinuity.» According to Buchloh, this gave rise to the «epistemology of archival order»[11]: A «collection of individual photographs, which as a whole 1920s affords insight into the complexity of a given subject.»[12] On the one hand, however, Sabiene Autsch does not use found image material, but her own photos (which in turn may contain found image material in collaged form). On the other hand, it is by no means about an «insight» into a «given subject», but rather about the creation of *formal series* that connect the individual images in different ways and traverse them. The «subject» is therefore not located on the level of content, but on that of form. The images are not connected by an iconography (as Buchloh describes for Broodthaer's absurd collections on the subject of «eagles»), nor by an iterative permutation, as in the photographs of industrial architectures by Bernd and Hilla Becher. Here a different episteme of archi val order is tested, one that takes the images seriously *as images* and not as signs that refer iconically and indexically to real-world occurrences. The «archival order» tested here establishes an archive of formal series that connects pictures by Sabiene Autsch from different periods and places. But, one could critically object: Is this not a relapse into a hypostasis of authorial subjectivity? Doesn't the exclusive use of her own images (instead of found visual material) undermine «the ‹anti-subjectivity› motif as a driving force in the collage aesthetic»?[13] Certainly, the authorial subject is not dispersed in Sabiene Autsch's work through the montage of heterogeneous and, above all, found visual material. In such a montage, the quoted images speak with a different voice, so to speak, and undermine the coherence of the author's voice. But even when confronted with found visual material, the con-

9 Foucault, Michel: Archaeology of Knowledge. New York: Pantheon 1972, p. 7.

10 Buchloh, Benjamin H. D.: Warburg's Paragon? The End of Collage/photomontage in Post-war Europe, in: Schaffner, Ingrid (eds.): Deep Storage. Munich: Prestel 1998, pp. 50–60, here p. 52.

11 Ibid., p. 54.

12 Ibid., p. 55.

13 Ibid, p. 53.

stellating author-subject still remains in a position of structuring power. Sabiene Autsch's strategy is more radical: she emphasizes that the elements that connect the photographs and collages into series are not inherent in the production of the images. Rather, they only become visible in the reflected practice of constellation, i.e. in the arrangement and rearrangement, in the compilation and exhibition as a micro-archive. In other words, Autsch makes series visible that she, as the author of the pictures, was not even aware of. «I don't see myself myself seeing.»[14] Each photo is a very conscious act and yet something creeps into the picture. The artist's unconscious appears in the series and traverses images from different times and places. The unconscious, as Deleuze has argued, is itself «differential and iterative by nature; it is serial, problematic and questioning.»[15] As serial, it can only appear in series. The subject of the montage is not «given», as Buchloh argues, but only emerges from the constellation of images. It appears in the tension between the pictures.

This unconscious should not be understood as a process of repression and forgetting traumatic experiences. Rather, it is an optical unconscious[16], a structure that initially pervades the visible unnoticed: An orange shape in a collage – a circle in the stone floor in a photograph – a central door of a similar color ... later a red circle appears ... Or: Grid-like structures of a stair railing – just such structures in a warehouse and on a promenade ... at the bottom of a swimming pool, in a drawing, in light and shadow in a forest ... Or: The color green ... very different images that combine in their structure of a series ...

«Experience and Structure,» the title of a monograph by Friedrich Kambartel from 1976, as part of a collage, sums it up: our experience is constantly shaped by unconscious serial structures that only become visible in the artistic constellation in the micro-archive of the exhibition or catalog. In this way, Autsch alienates our view of the everyday. She removes all closure from experience and makes its voids visible. Waldenfels once suggested speaking of «a pictoriality in things that precedes the pictoriality of images.»[17] Sabiene Autsch constellates images in order to make this original pictoriality visible again in the series. Here, the whole is more than the sum of the parts. Sabiene Autsch immerses herself in the visible, even dissolves into it, in order to allow us to experience the structure.

14 Därmann, Iris: Tod und Bild. Eine phänomenologische Mediengeschichte. Munich: Fink 1995, p. 409. My translation.

15 Deleuze, Gilles: Difference and Repetition. New York: Columbia University Press 1994, p. 108.

16 Cf. Krauss, Rosalind: The Optical Unconscious. Cambridge/MA: MIT Press 1993.

17 Waldenfels, Bernhard: Spiegel, Spur und Blick. Zur Genese des Bildes, in: Böhm, Gottfried (ed.): Homo Pictor. Munich: Saur 2001, pp. 14–31, here p. 20. My translation.

Flecker Hotel
2

AUSGANG
SHOP

2630ES
JLG
www.jlg.com
PRIDE
JLG

Den Troper

Hunde
schlafenden
Den Tropen

0-24

0-24

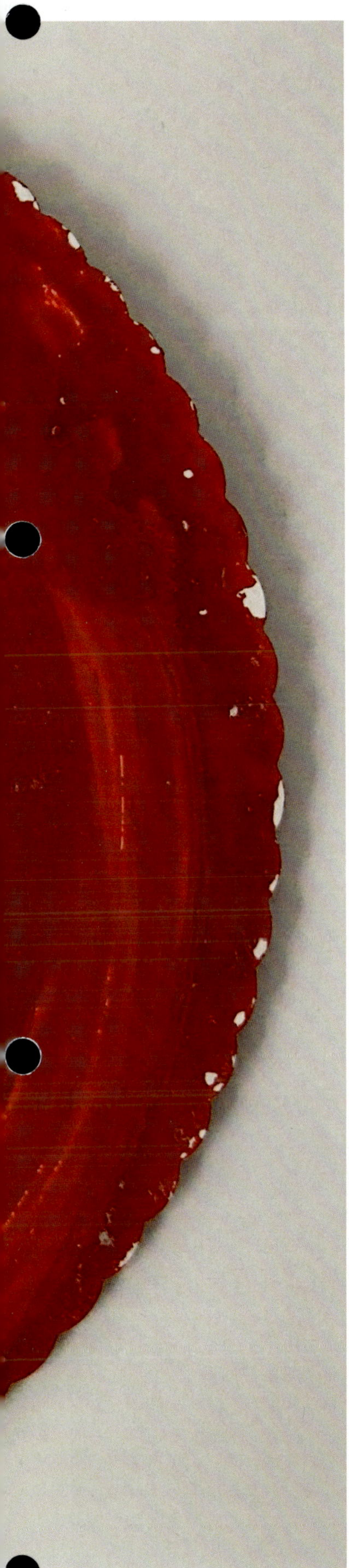

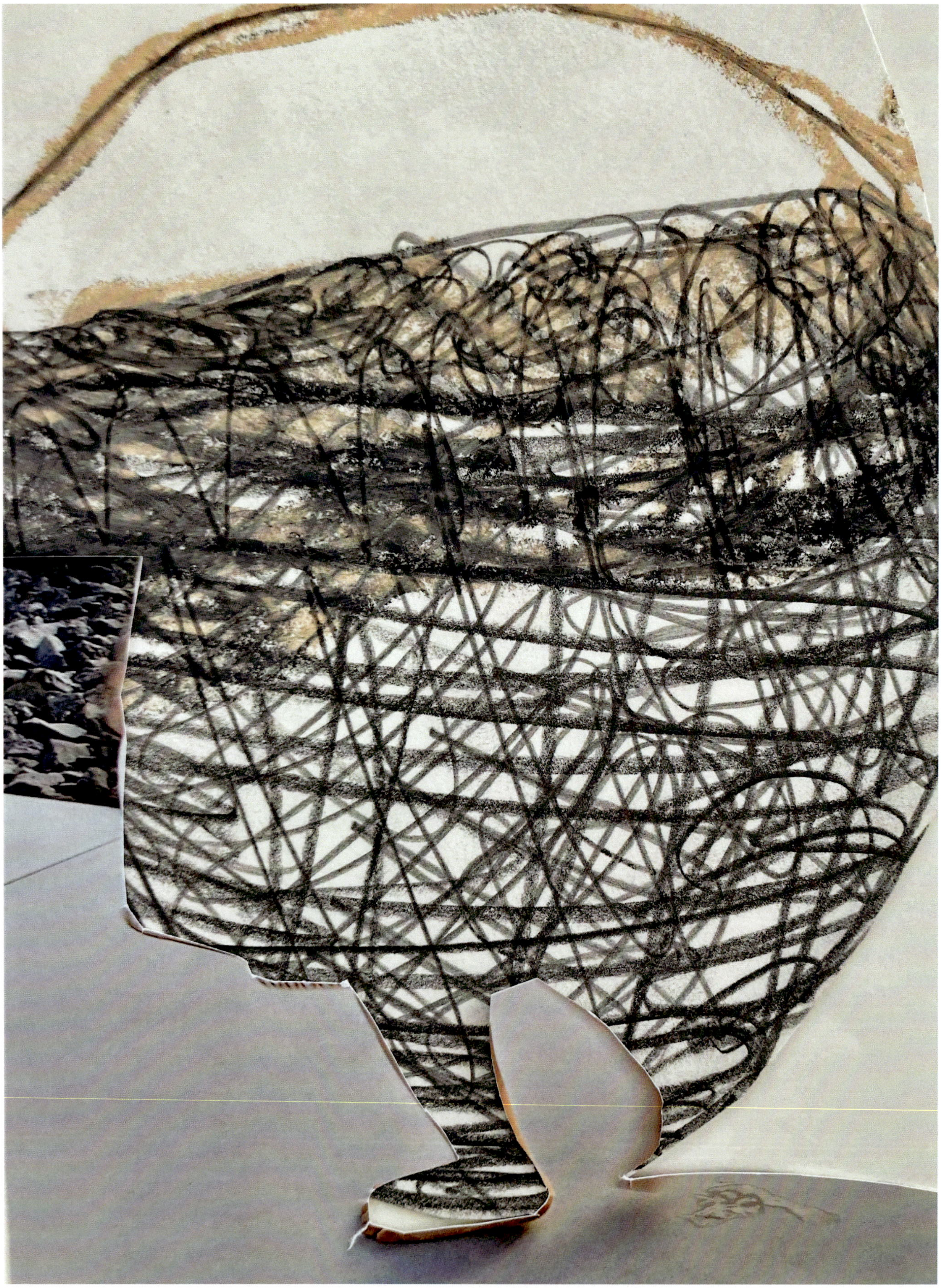

Michael Kröger

Was [nicht] zusammenpasst
Konstellationen im Werk von Sabiene Autsch

«Das Publikum wollte mehr. [...] Sie wünschten neue Wünsche. [...] Eine neue Sehnsucht.» (Martin Disler 1983)[1]

«Betasten und Durchreflektieren» – Zwischen Konstellation und Essay

Manchmal bestechen Kunstwerke durch Leichtigkeit *und* Ernsthaftigkeit, wodurch sie ihren Weg in die Kunstwelt finden. Experimentierend arbeitet und schreibt, wer seine Gegenstände «hin und her wälzt, befragt, betastet, prüft, durchreflektiert, wer von verschiedenen Seiten auf ihn losgeht, und in seinem Geistesblick sammelt, was er sieht und verwortet.» Diese Beschreibung der Aktivitäten des Essayisten, aus der Feder von Max Bense (1947), steht in denkbar engster Beziehung zur *Konstellation*, jener – gerade auch von Adorno hochgeschätzten – lebendig-produktiven Kategorie, die vorsichtig tastend Geistiges beschreibt.[2] Die experimentierend-offene Arbeitsweise von Sabiene Autsch und einige der hier vorgestellten Konstellationen sind in diesem essayistisch motivierten Sinne buchstäblich und metaphorisch als reflexive Befragungen, als materialbezogene Tastversuche und als zeitlos geformte Akte eines bildhaften Konstellierens zu begreifen. Ihre Bild-Zusammenstellungen oszillieren dabei zwischen Knappheit und Konstruktion, Anspruch und Assoziation, denen wir als anteilnehmende SpurenleserInnen eines «konstruierten Nebeneinanders»[3] folgen können.

Die Wahrnehmung eines Bildes verwandelt die Beziehung der Betrachtenden zu sich selbst und ihrer jeweiligen Örtlichkeit. Zwischen weiteren Bildern entstehen plötzlich neue Nachbarschaften und verändern bisherige Gewohnheiten unseres Blicks, der früher mehr auf Bedeutungen, jetzt jedoch eher auf Form- oder Strukturveränderungen achtet. Verkörpert die Begegnung mit einem Kunstwerk nicht einen exklusiven geistigen Ausnahmezustand, oder eine soziale Anpassungsleistung an eine Erfahrung, die heute zur Gewohnheit im «Betriebssystem Kunst» geworden ist? Die Bild-Zusammenstellungen von Sabiene Autsch wirken weniger als «Tatorte» von Vergangenem, als vielmehr wie geistesgegenwärtige Treffpunkte; Mach-Werke zwischen einem halbbewussten Machen, das oftmals wie gebastelt und bruchstückhaft wirkt und dem verwandelnden Erfinden immer neu beginnender Zugänge auf Seiten von uns, den gerade Rezipierenden. Das, was zwischen

1 Zitiert nach Bätschmann, Oskar: Das Kunstpublikum. Eine kurze Geschichte. Berlin: Hatje Cantz Verlag 2023, S. 9.

2 S. ausführlicher Adorno, Theodor W.: Der Essay als Form, in: Ders.: Noten zur Literatur I (1958). Aktualisierte Aufl., Frankfurt/M.: Suhrkamp Verlag 2022, S. 9–49, hier S. 36.

3 Ebd., S. 47.

den Bildern und besonders zwischen mehreren, in Beziehung zueinander gesetzten Bildern passiert, wird zum zeitbedingten Rohstoff meiner eigenen Wahrnehmung und unserer permanent vergleichenden, kollektiven Fantasie.

Effekte des Vergleichens

Was bringt eine Konstellation durch sich selbst als Form hervor?

Ein Mehrwert einer jeweils konstellativ erzeugten Zusammenstellung mehrerer disparater Elemente entsteht mit der Erkenntnis, dass hier *Gegenläufiges als Ineinander* gefügt ist. Der Anschein einer fotografisch fixierten Wirklichkeit wird aufgebrochen und an die unendlichen Möglichkeiten einer nächsten Begegnung mit ihren Betrachtenden angeschlossen. Ein Sinn des künstlerischen Machens von Sabiene Autsch findet als Konstellation formalen Ausdruck und zugleich visuelle Zuspitzung. In der vierteiligen fotografischen Arbeit «Plastics Mint (Basel)» von 2022 oszillieren Referenzen von Wirklichkeiten durch fragmentierte gelbe Bodenmarkierungen in ein verwirrendes Spiel mit Formen, Fläche und Strukturen, die sich permanent gegenseitig ins Wort zu fallen scheinen. Durch das Konstellieren, also das Zusammenstellen der Fotografien zu einer Serie, als Block oder dichte Hängung, entsteht ein kunstgewordener Zusammenhang, der buchstäblich passt und nicht passt. Zeitbedingte Nähe und scheinbar aus der Distanz beobachtetes Zeitloses existieren hier eng nebeneinander.

Konstellationen leben vom bewussten oder unbewussten Vergleichbarmachen: Ein durch Konstellationen realisiertes Vergleichen entwertet einerseits das jeweils miteinander Verglichene oder Jetzt-in-Beziehung-Gesetzte und führt andererseits zu Neubewertungen des bisher Unbearbeiteten. Luhmanns alte und heute immer drängender gestellte Frage der Moderne – *Wie wäre alles, was gemacht ist, auch noch anders möglich?* – wird im Medium der Konstellation gespiegelt: Bilder als Gegenwart gewordene Fragen triggern ihre jeweils eigenen Wirklichkeiten.

Die Frage der Vergleichbarkeit von (mindestens) zwei Bildern führt dabei unweigerlich und unerwartet zugleich in Dimensionen des Moralischen: Was sehe ich hier und jetzt, wenn ich zwei einzigartige oder nicht-einzigartige Bilder miteinander vergleiche und damit bewusst neu bewerte? Welche Dimensionen sehe und erkenne ich jetzt? Welche werde ich viel später in meinem Leben sehen und erkennen, die ich damals (also jetzt) möglicherweise übersehen habe? Konstellationen leben von Momenten des Triggerns und Getriggertwerdens. Ihr Kontext ereignet sich, wie in der mehrteiligen Collagearbeit «Den Tropen» (2023), durch einen fragmentierten Text-Kommentar. Begriffsfragmente funktionieren dabei wie ein Bild, zugleich auch als Assoziationstrigger. Dazwischen eröffnet sich eine Leerstelle: Ein immer auch aufblitzender, irritierend hellsichtiger Moment von etwas Emphatisch-Sinnlichem, was die Rezipierenden in gleichsam körperlicher Resonanz verspüren, wie etwa eine große rote Blüte auf dem weißen Kleid in unserer unscharf gewordenen Erinnerung (s. «Sommerkleid» von 2023). Demgegenüber steht «Whitney Potteries», eine mehrteilige fotografische Arbeit von 2023. Darin nehmen wir teil am klar organisierten Aufbau eines Ausstellungsdisplays, der sich vor dem Museum, hier das Whitney Museum of American Art in New York, realisiert und wie eine Allegorie auf das nicht-selbstverständliche Kunstsystem gelesen werden kann. Steht der Hubwagen für das ästhetisch Natürliche einer technischen Infrastruktur[4], so kann das aufwändige Stellagesystem als Metapher für eine modernistische, ästhetische Exklusivität verstanden werden, mit der hier auf ein Ereignis im musealen Raum verwiesen wird. Komplex ist dabei aber nicht nur ein spekulierender Sachverhalt, sondern auch der Anspruch, den mein eigener Blick gegenüber dem Konstellierten formuliert und damit etwas Zusätzliches, Kunstgewordenes in die Welt setzt. Eine seltsame Doppelung aus ästhetischer Konstruktion als einer gleichsam sich selbst rezipierenden Offenbarung von Kunstrealität?

... auch noch anders möglich?

Konstellationen operieren in ihren Zwischenwelten als temporäre Akte ihrer eigenen Bewusstwerdung. Sie ermöglichen während ihrer Rezeption die Auflösung von Gewohnheiten, die uns einerseits noch als Fotografien wie selbstverständlich erscheinen und andererseits schon als Bild, als Form einer künstlichen/fiktiven Zusammenstellung von etwas offenbaren, was sich dem vorschnell deuten wollenden Blick entziehen möchte. Gegensätzliches wird, wie in den künstlerischen Beispielen von Sabiene Autsch angedeutet, formal so gesteigert, dass es einen Mehrwert eines Bewusstmachens zur Geltung bringt. Je tiefliegender dieser dabei die Spannung, die eine Konstellation in der Tiefe des Materials hinterlässt, desto variantenreicher die Möglichkeiten, die es an der Oberfläche zum Ausdruck bringt.

Der Vorteil einer Konstellation entsteht mit den Fragen, die diese in den Rezipierenden auslösen –und die letztlich kein Ende finden. Auf diese Weise lebt die Konstellation durch das Momenthafte, in Akten von passiver Aktivität – was unsere Wahrnehmung in einen mäandernden Fluss zu verwandeln scheint ... *Immer auch wäre etwas auch noch anders möglich*: Aus diesem weithin geöffneten Mantra der späten Moderne entsteht eine jeweils neu zu konstellierende Neufügung, die sich ihrerseits aus Wirklichkeiten als Effekte von Konstruktionen und Spekulationen ihres Verändertwerdens ableiten. Als Teil einer visuellen Gruppierung (Konstellation) kann eine Unsichtbarkeit zwischen den Bildern selbstbestimmt geistreich weiter genutzt werden, muss es aber nicht; es kann gleichzeitig auch einen fremdbestimmten Machtbereich dazwischen markieren: Irgendwo zwischen Obsessionen des Faktischen und systemischer Störung des Fiktiven, zwischen Erinnerung und fremd gewordener Gegenwart, zwischen ästhetisch funktionierender Inkorrektheit und frei flottierender, technischer Selbstverständlichkeit eines sich selbst bestimmenden Machens ...

4 Vgl. dazu van Brevern, Jan: Das natürliche Kunstwerk. Zur Ästhetisierung von Natürlichkeit im 18. Jahrhundert. Konstanz: Wallstein Verlag 2023, S. 102.

Michael Kröger

What [Does Not] Fit Together
Constellations in the work of Sabiene Autsch

«The audience wanted more. [...] They wanted new wishes. [...] A new longing.» (Martin Disler 1983)[1]

«Touching and reflecting» – between constellation and essay

Sometimes works of art are characterised by lightness *and* seriousness, which is how they find their way into the art world. Those who work and write experimentally are those who «roll their objects back and forth, question them, touch them, examine them, reflect on them, approach them from different angles and collect what they see and analyse in their mind's eye.» This description of the essayist's activities, penned by Max Bense (1947), has the closest possible relationship to the *constellation,* the living-productive category – highly valued by Adorno in particular – that describes the spiritual in a cautiously tentative way.[2] In this essayistically motivated sense, Sabiene Autsch's experimental and open working method and some of the constellations presented here are to be understood literally and metaphorically as reflexive questioning, as material-related tactile experiments and as timelessly formed acts of pictorial constellation. Her image compilations oscillate between brevity and construction, claim and association, which we can follow as participating readers of traces of a «constructed coexistence».[3]

The perception of an image transforms the viewer's relationship to themselves and their respective location. New neighbourhoods suddenly emerge between further images and change the previous habits of our gaze, which used to pay more attention to meanings, but now pays more attention to changes in form or structure. Does the encounter with a work of art not embody an exclusive mental state of exception, or a social adaptation to an experience that has now become a habit in the «art operating system»? Sabiene Autsch's compositions of images seem less like «crime scenes» of the past and more like meeting points of the mind; works of making between a semi-conscious making that often seems tinkered and fragmentary and the transforming invention of ever new approaches on the part of us, the recipients. What happens between the pictures and especially between several pictures placed in relation to each other becomes the time-dependent raw material of my own perception and our permanently comparing, collective imagination.

1 Quoted from Bätschmann, Oskar: Das Kunstpublikum. A short history. Berlin: Hatje Cantz Verlag 2023, p. 9.

2 See in more detail Adorno, Theodor W.: Der Essay als Form, in: Ders.: Noten zur Literatur I (1958). Updated edition, Frankfurt/M.: Suhrkamp Verlag 2022, pp. 9–49, here p. 36.

3 Ibid, p. 47.

Effects of comparison

What does a constellation produce through itself as a form?

The added value of a constellation of several disparate elements is created with the realisation that *opposites are* joined *together* here. The appearance of a photographically fixed reality is broken up and connected to the infinite possibilities of a next encounter with the viewer. A sense of artistic making by Sabiene Autsch finds formal expression as a constellation and at the same time visual intensification. In the four-part photographic work «Plastics Mint (Basel)» from 2022, references to realities oscillate through fragmented yellow floor markings in a confusing game with forms, surfaces and structures that seem to constantly interfere with each other. By constellating the photographs into a series, as a block or hanging, an artistic context is created that literally fits and does not fit. Time-related proximity and the seemingly timeless, observed from a distance, exist side by side here.

Constellations live from consciously or unconsciously making comparisons: On the one hand, a comparison realised through constellations devalues what has been compared or what is now in relation to each other and, on the other hand, leads to re-evaluations of what has not yet been processed. Luhmann's old and today increasingly urgent question of modernity – *How would everything that is made be possible in a different way?* – is mirrored in the medium of the constellation: Images as questions that have become present trigger their own realities.

The question of the comparability of (at least) two images inevitably and unexpectedly leads to dimensions of morality: What do I see here and now when I compare two unique or non-unique images with each other and thus consciously re-evaluate them? What dimensions do I see and recognise now? Which ones will I see and recognise much later in my life that I may have overlooked at the time (i.e. now)? Constellations live from moments of triggering and being triggered. Their context occurs, as in the multi-part collage work «Den Tropen» (2023), through a fragmented text commentary. Fragments of terms function like an image, but also as a trigger for association. In between, a blank space opens up: a constantly flashing, irritatingly clairvoyant moment of something emphatic and sensual, which the recipients feel in a kind of physical resonance, such as a large red blossom on the white dress in our blurred memory (see «Sommerkleid» from 2023). In contrast, there is «Whitney Potteries», a multi-part photographic work from 2023, in which we take part in the clearly organised construction of an exhibition display, which is realised in front of the museum, in this case the Whitney Museum of American Art in New York, and can be read as an allegory of the non-self-evident art system. If the pallet truck stands for the aesthetically natural aspects of a technical infrastructure[4], the elaborate storage system can be understood as a metaphor for a modernist, aesthetic exclusivity that refers to an event in the museum space. Complex, however, is not only a speculative fact, but also the claim that my own gaze formulates vis-à-vis the constellation and thus places something additional, something that has become art in the world. A strange doubling of aesthetic construction as a self-receiving revelation of art reality?

4 Cf. van Brevern, Jan: The natural work of art. On the aestheticisation of naturalness in the 18th century. Constance: Wallstein Verlag 2023, p. 102.

... also possible in other ways?

Constellations operate in their intermediate worlds as temporary acts of their own realisation. During their reception, they enable the dissolution of habits that, on the one hand, still seem self-evident to us as photographs and, on the other hand, already reveal themselves as images, as a form of an artificial/fictive composition of something that would like to elude the hastily interpretative gaze. As indicated in the artistic examples, opposites are formally heightened in such a way that they emphasise an added value of awareness. The deeper the tension that a constellation leaves behind in the depths of the material, the more varied the possibilities that it expresses on the surface.

The advantage of a constellation arises with the questions that it triggers in the recipients – and which ultimately find no end. In this way, the constellation lives through the momentary, in acts of passive activity – which seems to transform our perception into a meandering flow ... *Something else would always be possible as well*: from this wide-open mantra of late modernism, a new constellation emerges, which in turn derives from realities as effects of constructions and speculations of their being changed. As part of a visual grouping (constellation), an invisibility between the images can continue to be used in a self-determined and ingenious way, but it does not have to; at the same time, it can also mark an externally determined area of power in between: Somewhere between obsessions of the factual and systemic disruption of the fictive, between memory and a present that has become alien, between aesthetically functioning incorrectness and the free-floating, technical self-evidence of a self-determining making ...

RAM 1500 V8

Erfa
Stru

rung und
tur

5114
563

KAPULICA AG

KAPULICA AG
CA AG
KAPULICA AG

ZG 2113

LSU
TIGERS

„Ich war ein Einzelgänger“

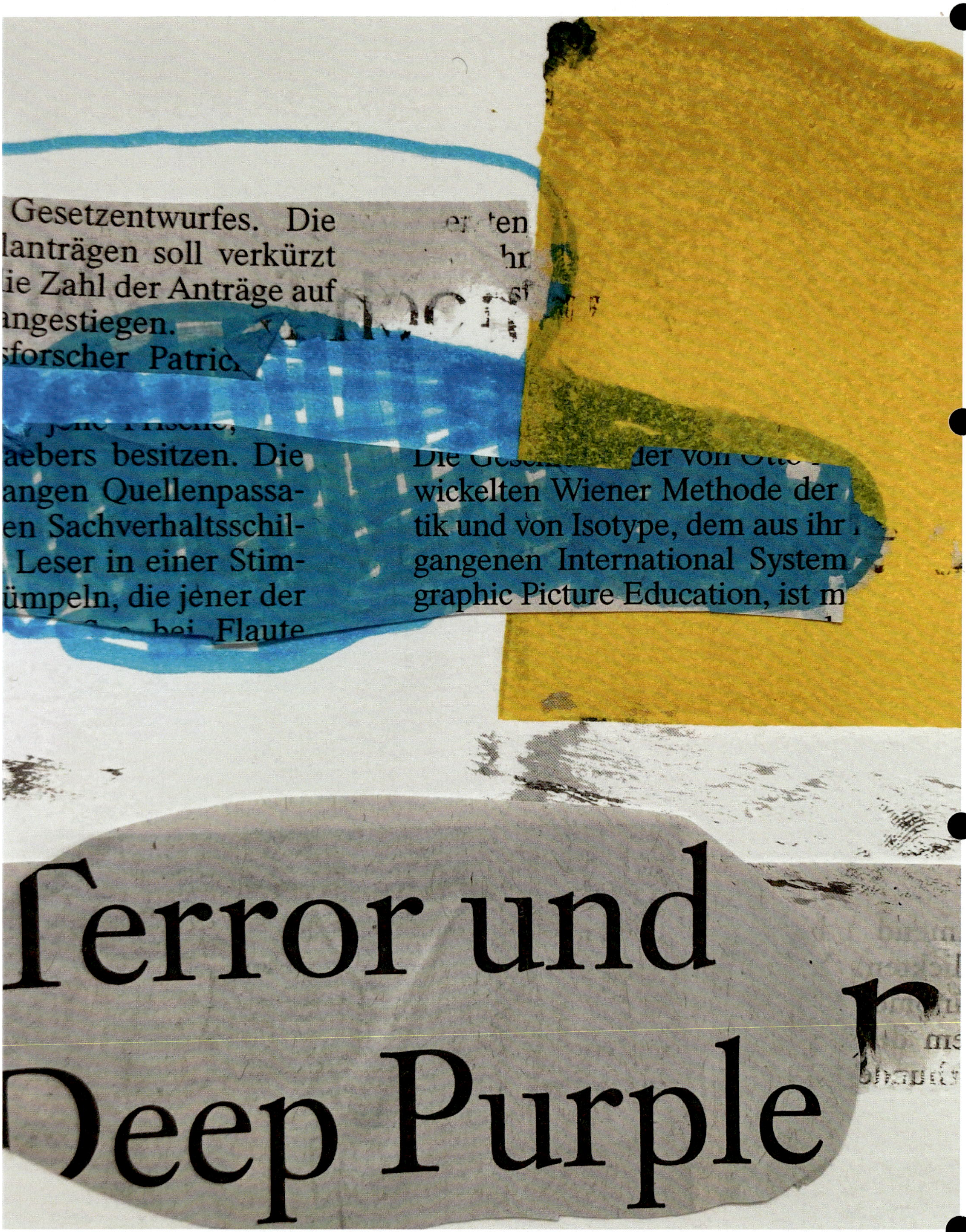
Gesetzentwurfes. Die
lanträgen soll verkürzt
ie Zahl der Anträge auf
angestiegen.
sforscher Patric
aebers besitzen. Die
angen Quellenpassa-
en Sachverhaltsschil-
Leser in einer Stim-
ümpeln, die jener der
Flaute
wickelten Wiener Methode der
tik und von Isotype, dem aus ihr
gangenen International System
graphic Picture Education, ist m
Terror und
Deep Purple

GlaubE
BBL

Gefühl,

BAY CRANE

Sabiene Autsch

Professorin für Kunst, Kunstgeschichte und ihre Didaktik, Universität Paderborn.

2008 Habilitation an der Universität/Kunsthochschule Kassel mit einer Untersuchung zur Rezeptionsgeschichte kuratorischer Positionen und Ausstellungen der 1920er bis 1990er Jahre.

2006–08 Vertretungsprofessur im Fach Kunst, Universität Paderborn.

2002–04 Wissenschaftliche Mitarbeiterin an der Universität/Kunsthochschule Kassel, DFG-Projekt «Expositionen».

1998 Promotion (Dr. phil.) an der Universität Siegen mit einer Untersuchung zur Generationengeschichte und Kunstpolitik im 20. Jahrhundert. 1. und 2. Staatsexamen. Studium der Kunst, Kunstgeschichte, Neuere und Neueste Geschichte, Soziologie und Pädagogik an den Universitäten Siegen und Wien.

Auszeichnungen Forschungsstipendium des Landes Nordrhein-Westfalen, «Visual History» (1994/95)
Forschungspreis der Camilla-Dirlmeier-Stiftung für das Studien- und Ausstellungsprojekt «Der Krieg als Reise» (1998)

Lehr- und Forschungsschwerpunkte

Kunstgeschichte und Kunsttheorie 19.–21. Jahrhundert, Künstlerische Strategien der Gegenwartskunst, Geschichte der Documenta, Museums- und Ausstellungstheorien, Studio Studies, Artistic/Curatorial Research, Mikroformate, Kunst und Kulinarik, Künstlerische Kunstvermittlung.

Seit 1990 eigene künstlerische Arbeiten (Druckgrafik, Fotografie, Zeichnung, Mixed Media), Atelier und Mitglied der Ateliergemeinschaft Friedrichstraße Siegen. Kuratorische Projekte und Ausstellungen im institutionellen und nicht-institutionellen Raum u. a. 2024 Kunstverein Paderborn (G), 2022 Oberes Schloss Siegen (G), Atelierhaus Arlesheim/Basel (G), 2019 Art Galerie Siegen (E), 2014 Museum Dringenberg (E), 2008 Art Galerie Siegen (E), 2008 Kunstraum Schwerin (E), 2007 IHK-Galerie, Siegen (E), 2006 Yan-Huang Art Museum, Peking, VR China (G), Kunstmusem Deyang, VR China (G), 2005 Open Studio, Ateliers Siegen (G), 2004 Haus Oranienstraße, Siegen (G), 2003 Munwhailbo Gallery, Seoul, Korea (G).

Künstlerbücher und Kataloge (Auswahl)

Micro Archives. Mit Texten von Jens Schröter und Michael Kröger. Edition Imorde Berlin 2024. Bis hierin und weiter. Hundert Jahre Arbeitsgemeinschaft Siegerländer Künstlerinnen und Künstler. Hg. v. Arbeitsgemeinschaft Siegerländer Künstlerinnen und Künstler, Siegen 2022, S. 84–87. Walk With Me. Mit einem Textauszug von Raimar Zons. Siegen 2022. Sabiene Autsch. Arbeiten 2004–2014. Paderborn 2014. Dem Auge Unerhörtes bieten. Mit einem Text von Jens Schröter, IHK Siegen, 2007. In turn. global exhibition project. Hg. von Arbeitsgemeinschaft Siegerländer Künstler (ASK). Seoul/ Siegen 2006. Sternzeichen Jungfrau. Bild- und Textlektüren von Sabiene Autsch. Siegen 2006. Für Erwachsene und Jugendliche. Mit einem Vorwort von Florian Prinz. Siegen/ Berlin 2004.

Bilder/Plates